499
CASH

D0292156

# Rice

# Rice

*Seventy-eight*

*Recipes for*

*Arborio,*

*Basmati,*

*Brown,*

*Jasmine,*

*White,*

*and Wild*

*Rice*

by
Bonnie Tandy Leblang
and Joanne Lamb Hayes

Harmony Books/New York

Published by Harmony Books, a division of Crown Publishers, Inc., 201 East 50th Street, New York, New York 10022. Member of the Crown Publishing Group.

HARMONY and colophon are trademarks of Crown Publishers, Inc.

Manufactured in the United States of America

Library of Congress Cataloging-in-Publication Data

Leblang, Bonnie Tandy.
Rice/by Bonnie Tandy Leblang and Joanne Lamb Hayes.
p.    cm.
1. Cookery (Rice)   I. Hayes, Joanne Lamb.   II. Title.
TX 809.R5L43    1991
641.6'318—dc20                                                        90-31247
CIP

ISBN 0-517-57694-5

Book design by Linda Kocur

Illustrations by Jennifer Harper

10   9   8   7   6   5   4   3   2

# contents

# acknowledgments

Many thanks to The USA Rice Council for
Market Development, especially Kris O'Brien,
for her help and enthusiastic support.
Thanks to Harriet Bell for giving us the chance.
Thanks to Dorothy Lamb for her
encouragement and allowing messes in
her kitchen. Thanks to the late
Lucille Tandy for her confidence and
moral support. And, thanks to
Bryan, Eric, Heather, and Claire, our kids,
for their particular palates.

# Rice

# introduction

Rice is, without question, the world's grain of choice. More people eat rice as the staple of their diet than any other single food. Even those of us who don't live by rice alone are eating more of it than ever before. Now readily available in more varieties with innovative ways to prepare them, rice offers comfort (Red Beans and Rice and Rice Pudding) or elegance (Wild Rice and Mushroom Soup or Saffron Rice Timbales); culinary tradition (Risotto and Arroz con Pollo); or inventive creations (Rice Cheesecake and Wild Rice Pancakes with Caviar).

Because of the ease of preparation and the ability to keep its flavor and texture after it is cooked, rice has become a home-cooking staple as well as one of the most frequently served side dishes in restaurants. Rice is nutritious, inexpensive, versatile, quick or slow to prepare depending on your mood, and always delicious, whether it is served as an accompaniment or as the main ingredient of a dish. In these pages you will find traditional favorites and new ideas for preparing this time-honored grain in everything from soup to dessert.

1

# A Grain of Truth

Rice has been part of civilization for so long that its origins have been difficult to trace. It isn't known for certain whether it first appeared in India, China, or Thailand, but it was certainly in an area where there is a great deal of rain followed by a dry season. For centuries this wild grass was resown in the same swampy areas where it was originally found, and production was dependent entirely upon the will of nature. Then the Chinese found that when fields were artificially flooded for rice cultivation, the crops increased. Despite efforts to keep these methods a secret, rice cultivation spread to Japan and the Middle East. The Western world probably came in contact with rice about 335 B.C., when Alexander the Great's soldiers entered India and saw rice fields. There is no clear record, though, of the use of rice in Europe until the fourteenth century.

Rice came to America as early as 1647, when Sir William Berkeley planted half a bushel of seed on his land in Virginia. Rice cultivation didn't attract much attention until more than forty years later, when it was introduced into South Carolina. There are several stories about the coming of rice to the Carolinas. Some date it to 1685, when a Captain John Thurber and his ship full of rice was blown off course and arrived at Charleston. Others claim that it was a Dutch ship from Madagascar, far off its course to Liverpool, which first gave the grain to South Carolina planters in 1694. Or perhaps the arrival of a hundred-pound bag of rice from someone named Ashby in London started the industry. But whatever it was, the rice industry soon flourished in the Carolinas, and by the end of the seventeenth century, America was exporting rice to England and other parts of Europe.

America's history and the story of rice are interrelated at many points. During the revolutionary war, the British occupied the Charleston area and sent all the harvested rice back to Britain, leaving none for seed. Food had always been one of Thomas Jefferson's passions. On a diplomatic mission to Italy in 1787, he discovered the high-quality rice growing in Italy, and he smuggled some of the seed back to the struggling Carolina industry. Despite Jefferson's help, the rice industry gradually left Carolina's wetlands for the fertile Mississippi Valley, where the fields could be flooded during the growing season and then dried out for mechanical harvesting.

## Rice Nutrition
■

*Rice is so nutritious that for one half of the world's population, it is not just their staple carbohydrate, but the major portion of their total diet. Brown rice provides calcium, phosphorus, potassium, niacin, fiber, and vitamin E as well as complex carbohydrates. While milled white rice is lower in these nutrients, because the bran layer has been removed, most rice produced in the United States is enriched with these nutrients. Imported rice is not.*

*Rice is the first grain given to newborn babies because it's* nonallergenic *and easy to digest. Rice is* gluten-free. *(Some people are allergic to gluten, the protein found in wheat.) Rice is* cholesterol-free *and has only a trace of fat. A ½ cup serving ranges from 80 calories for parboiled to 85 calories for brown rice.*

# "Wild" perhaps, but certainly not "rice."

When early explorers reached America's Great Lakes, they discovered Native Americans harvesting and eating the aquatic grass *Zizania aquatica*. Because it was growing in shallow water and resembled European rice, they called it "Wild rice" or "Indian rice." Ojibway or Chippewa Native Americans still harvest some of America's rice from riverbanks in the Great Lakes region that were seeded with the grain by their ancestors. Wild rice is harvested into canoes by bending the stalks of grain over the canoe and beating them with sticks to knock the seeds into the boat. A great many seeds fall back into the river and reseed the area to produce next year's crop.

Wild rice is now being produced commercially in paddys, both in the Great Lakes area and

## Rice and Cholesterol
■

*Current research has shown that rice bran may in fact be more effective in lowering blood cholesterol than oat bran. (Rice bran has almost double the nutrients as oat bran.) While scientists are still trying to isolate the components responsible for cholesterol lowering, they believe it is not the soluble fiber in the rice that's responsible. In oat bran, apples, and legumes, it is the soluble fiber that's been touted for its cholesterol-lowering effects.*

*β-sitosterol, one of many naturally occurring components in rice bran oil, has been found to help lower cholesterol. Rice bran oil is a concentrated source of β-sitosterol, although β-sitosterol naturally occurs in many vegetables or grains.*

*Researchers think the components of the oil work*

(continued)

4

in California. Native American producers who harvest it from the riverbanks claim that their lighter, greener, natural product has a far superior taste to the commercially produced dark variety. Producers of lake or paddy wild rice have responded by outproducing the native harvesters and selling their product at a reduced price.

With few exceptions rice is rice, and *any* rice can be used for *any* cooking purpose. Various cultures look for different characteristics in their rice. Americans prefer rice that is fluffy and doesn't stick together when cooked, while some other cultures prefer rice that is soft and sticky. Rice is classified as long *(indica)* or medium and short *(japonica)* depending on the ratio of its length to width. It is also classified by cooking characteristics.

Usually, American long grain rice results in a fluffy product with separate grains when cooked, while medium and short

*by reducing the absorption of cholesterol in the blood and by decreasing the production of cholesterol by the liver. The rice bran oil components reduce the "bad" cholesterol—the low density lipoproteins (LDLs) while having no effect on the "good" cholesterol—the high density lipoproteins (HDLs).*

*Other rice bran components thought to have cholesterol-lowering properties include tocotrienols, oryzanols, β-glucan, and hemicelluloses.*

grain rice produce a stickier product. In some recipes, we suggest a specific rice to make a traditional dish. Don't feel limited to our suggestions; except in rice pudding and risotto, try using any rice you have on hand. The results will be different but just as delicious. Adjust the liquid and cooking time, if necessary, according to the package instructions. Parboiled, blended, and brown rice each take longer to cook and often need more liquid than traditional white rice.

# A Rice Glossary

*Arborio:* A medium grain rice imported from Italy, mainly used in risotto (see page 80). When a risotto technique is used for cooking, the rice is creamy on the outside and al dente— firm to the bite—on the inside.

*Aromatic Rice:* Brown or white rice with a fragrant corn or nutlike aroma and flavor. The flavor component comes from 2-acetyl

## Tips for perfect rice
■

• *Always measure the rice and liquid accurately. Then cook it following the recipe instructions.*

• *Do not stir. Stirring rice releases its starch, making the rice sticky. Stir only if the recipe says to.*

• *Fluff the rice with a fork before serving. This allows the steam to escape and helps keep the grains separated.*

• *Cook rice shortly before serving. If it's necessary to hold rice for a short period of time, place a tea towel over the pot and then cover it. A tea towel absorbs the condensation from steam, instead of letting it fall back into the rice, which can make the rice gummy.*

• *Rice that has been stored in a dry area for a long time may need a longer cooking period.*

• *Cooking rice in high concentrations of acid, such as*

(continued)

pyroline, a compound naturally found in all rice as well as in corn and nuts. This flavor compound is ten times higher in concentration in aromatic rice than in nonaromatic. Some common imported varieties include Basmati and Jasmine. U.S. aromatics are commercially available as Texmati, Delta Rose, Della Gourmet, popcorn rice, Wild Pecan, and Wehani rice. Aromatic properties vary from year to year, just like fine wines. If it's a good year for the rice and it is stored in a cool, dry place, the aromatic properties will improve with age. This occurs in both the milled and unmilled state.

*Basmati:* Aromatic rice imported from India or Pakistan; the name means "queen of fragrance."

*Blended:* A commercial mixture of many varieties of rice, some of which have different-colored bran layers. May include black, red, and orange, along with sev-

*tomatoes or orange juice, inhibits the rice's ability to take in water. You may need extra liquid, and possibly extra time, when cooking in these liquids.*

## Using leftover rice

■

• *Since long grain rice can become hard when refrigerated (retrogradation), reheat leftover rice in 2 tablespoons of water over low heat until warm.*
• *Leftover rice freezes well. Pack it into 1 cup portions, and freeze for up to 3 months.*
• *To reheat frozen, leftover rice in the microwave, add 2 tablespoons liquid to 1 cup rice, and cook at full power (100 percent) for 2 minutes.*

eral shades of brown rice. Wild rice is included in some blends.

*Bran:* The nutrient-rich layer removed in the milling process; commercially available for use in baked goods. Recent research indicates that rice bran—specifically the oil in the rice bran—may be more effective than oat bran in lowering blood cholesterol.

*Brown Rice:* Unmilled rice with the hull removed; may be various shades of brown, red, or black in color, contains the bran layer; available short, medium, or long grain; may be parboiled or instantized; also available partially milled with only a portion of the bran removed.

*Enriched:* A process used to restore some of the nutrients removed during manufacturing; 3.75 percent of the U.S. Recommended Daily Allowances of iron and 5 percent of the B-vitamins, thiamine, and niacin are added. Because it is manda-

## Troubleshooting

∎

If your rice grains are too firm:
• *you didn't add enough liquid or the liquid was too high in acid.*
• *the pan was too large and some of the water evaporated.*
• *the pan lid was too loose.*
• *you didn't cook it long enough.*
If your rice grains are too mushy:
• *you used too much liquid.*
• *you cooked it too long.*
If your rice grains are too sticky:
• *you used too much liquid.*
• *you stirred the rice during the cooking.*
• *you held it too long before serving.*

tory in some states, 90 percent of U.S. rice is enriched.

*Instant or Precooked Rice:* Instantized brown or white rice that is precooked, then dehydrated for rapid preparation.

*Jasmine:* Aromatic rice imported from Thailand. The uncooked grains are thin and long, producing a soft, sticky rice when cooked. Presently over 50 percent of all imported rice is Jasmine. U.S.-grown Jasmine will soon be available.

*Light or Micromilled:* Partially milled rice, light brown in color; some of the nutrient-rich bran layer remains. It cooks in about 20 minutes.

*Milling:* A process that removes the bran.

*Parboiled:* Often referred to as Converted®; a process in which the rice is steamed and pressurized to force the nutrients from the bran into the center, the endosperm, of the rice; it also hard-

## Storing Rice
■

*Store milled white, parboiled, or precooked rice in a tight container in a cool, dry location. Although it will keep almost indefinitely, it is best to use it within one year.*

*Brown rice, rice bran, rice polish, and any of the blended rices have a shorter shelf life because of the oil in the bran layer. Unopened, they will keep up to six months in a cool, dry location. Refrigeration or freezer storage is recommended for longer storage or in warm climates.*

ens the grain, so the resulting rice requires more water and a longer cooking time than non-parboiled rice. If cooked properly, the rice grains remain separate; they don't stick together even when kept warm for a short period of time, about 20 to 30 minutes, after cooking.

*Retrogradation:* The process in which cooked rice becomes hard again when refrigerated. This happens to rice high in the starch amylose, such as U.S. long grain rice.

*Rice (Oryza sativa):* Grown in long, medium, or short grain. Regular or aromatic.

*Rice Bran Oil:* A mild-flavored unsaturated oil, excellent for frying because of its very high smoking point; it can be heated to a high temperature before burning.

*Rice Couscous:* Cracked rice resembling couscous, a cracked wheat product.

*Rice Grits:* A cracked rice product resembling corn grits; can be used as a substitute for corn grits.

*Rice Flour:* A finely ground rice product resembling wheat flour. Contains no gluten; can be substituted for wheat flour only in products where structure is not needed. Do not use in muffins, breads, or cakes without also adding wheat flour.

*Rice Meal:* A finely cracked rice product similar to cornmeal; can be used in baking or for coating instead of cornmeal. To make, grind uncooked rice in a blender.

*Rice Polish:* A nutrient-rich, creamy-colored product produced in the final step of milling; contains some bran.

*Rough or Paddy Rice:* Rice in the hull, as it comes from the field.

*Sweet, Waxy, or Glutinous Rice:* A short grain white rice,

# Rice Cooking at a Glance

| Type | Liquid per 1 cup rice | Yield | Cooking Time Boiled | Microwave | Oven |
|------|------|------|------|------|------|
| Long grain white regular | 1¾–2 cups | 3 cups | 15 min. | 5 min. 100%; 15 min. 50% | 25–30 min. |
| Medium or short grain white | 1½–1¾ cups | 3 cups | 15 min. | 5 min. 100%; 15 min. 50% | 25–30 min. |
| Parboiled white | 2–2½ cups | 3–4 cups | 20–25 min. | 5 min. 100%; 20 min. 50% | 30–40 min. |
| Long grain brown | 2–2½ cups | 3–4 cups | 45–50 min. | 5 min. 100%; 45–55 min. 30% | 1 hour |
| American long grain aromatic | 1¾ cups | 3 cups | 15 min. | 5 min. 100%; 15 min. 50% | 25–30 min. |
| Wild rice | 3½ cups | 3–4 cups | 45–50 min. | 5 min. 100%; 45–55 min. 30% | 1 hour |
| Precooked, blends, mixes, and other rices | Follow package directions | | | | |

very sticky and slightly sweet in flavor when cooked, usually used for sushi and rice pudding.

*White Rice:* Milled rice with the hull and bran removed; available short, medium, or long grain; can be parboiled or instantized.

*Wild Rice (Zizania aquatica):* Not a true rice, the grain of an aquatic grass native to North America.

# basic rice recipes

# basic white rice

*Makes about 3 cups cooked rice*

■ *1.* If using imported rice, rinse the rice carefully several times and remove any small stones or impurities. This step is unnecessary for U.S.-grown rice.

■ *2.* Combine the rice with 2 cups water for long grain regular rice, 1¾ cups water for short or medium grain regular rice or 2½ cups water for parboiled rice with the butter and salt in a heavy 2-quart saucepan with lid.

■ *3.* Bring the rice mixture to a boil over high heat; reduce heat, cover, and cook 15 to 18 minutes or until the rice is tender and the liquid is absorbed. Fluff the rice with a fork and serve.

Note: For firmer rice, reduce the liquid by ¼ cup and cook for 15 minutes. For softer rice, increase the liquid by ¼ cup and cook for 20 minutes.

1 cup white rice (long, medium, or short grain; regular or parboiled)

1½ to 2½ cups water or broth

1 teaspoon butter, rice bran oil, or olive oil

½ to ¾ teaspoon salt to taste

**Oven Method:** Preheat the oven to 350°F. Bring the water to a boil. In a 1-quart casserole, combine the rice, boiling water, butter, and salt. Cover and bake 25 to 30 minutes, or until rice is tender and all the liquid is absorbed. Fluff with a fork and serve.

**Microwave Method:** In a 2-quart microwave-safe baking dish, combine the rice, water, butter, and salt. Cover and microwave at full power (100 percent) for 5 minutes or until the water boils. Then microwave for 15 minutes at medium power (50 percent) 20 minutes for parboiled. Fluff with a fork and serve.

If your oven power is less than 500 watts, see the manufacturer's instructions for cooking rice.

*While imported rice should always be rinsed before use, U.S.-grown rice shouldn't. Rinsing domestic rice removes some of the nutrients added during enrichment.*

# basic brown rice

*Makes about 3 cups cooked rice*

■ *1.* If using imported rice, rinse the rice carefully several times and remove any small stones or impurities. Do not rinse U.S.-grown rice.

■ *2.* Combine the brown rice, water, butter, and salt in a heavy 2-quart saucepan with a lid.

■ *3.* Bring the rice mixture to a boil over high heat; reduce heat, cover, and cook 45 to 50 minutes or until the rice is tender and the liquid is absorbed. Fluff the rice with a fork and serve.

**Oven Method:** Preheat the oven to 350°F. Bring the water to a boil. In a 1½-quart casserole, combine the rice, boiling water, butter, and salt. Cover and bake 55 to 60 minutes, or until the rice is tender and all the liquid is absorbed. Fluff with a fork and serve.

**1 cup brown rice**

**2½ cups water or broth**

**1 teaspoon butter, rice bran oil, or olive oil**

**½ to ¾ teaspoon salt to taste**

**Microwave Method:** In a 2-quart microwave-safe dish, combine the rice, water, butter, and salt. Cover and microwave at full power (100 percent) for 5 minutes or until the water boils. Then microwave at medium-low power (30 percent) for 45 to 50 minutes. Fluff with a fork and serve.

*Rice cookers are useful if you frequently cook rice for a crowd. However, the texture of the rice is slightly different from rice cooked by other methods. Rice can also be cooked in a steamer, but the basic boiled rice method is easier and less likely to produce broken grains and sticky rice.*

# basic wild rice

*Makes about 2½ cups cooked wild rice*

■ *1.* Rinse the rice thoroughly several times in cold water. Combine the wild rice, water, butter, and salt in a heavy 2-quart saucepan with a lid.
■ *2.* Bring the rice mixture to a boil over high heat; reduce heat, cover, and cook 45 to 50 minutes or until the rice is tender and the liquid is absorbed. Fluff with a fork and serve.

**Oven Method:** Preheat the oven to 350°F. Bring the water to a boil. In a 1½-quart casserole, combine the rice, boiling water, butter, and salt. Cover and bake 1 hour, or until the rice is tender and all the liquid is absorbed. Fluff with a fork and serve.

**Microwave Method:** In a 2-quart microwave-safe dish, combine the rice, water, butter, and salt. Cover and microwave at full power for 5 minutes or until the water boils. Then microwave at medium-low power (30 percent) for 45 to 50 minutes. Fluff with a fork and serve.

1 cup wild rice

3½ cups water or broth

1 teaspoon butter, rice bran oil, or olive oil

½ to ¾ teaspoon salt to taste

# soups and starters

*"When Japan's first nuclear ship, the Mutsu, developed a radioactive leak on its trial voyage, its engineers tried to stop the leakage with a paste made of boiled rice and neutron-absorbing boron crystals. It didn't work."*

*Waverley Root, Food, 1980*

# wild rice and mushroom soup

*If you have some leftover cooked wild rice on hand and can remember to soak the mushrooms ahead of time, this elegant soup can be ready in practically no time.*

*6 servings*

■ *1.* Pour the boiling water and 2 tablespoons of sherry over the dried mushrooms. Let stand for 3 hours, or until soft. Drain, reserving the liquid, and remove and discard the stems, then thinly slice the mushroom caps.
■ *2.* Heat the butter in a 4-quart saucepan over medium-high heat. Add and saute the onion, red pepper, celery, and mushrooms until the vegetables soften, about 5 minutes. Sprinkle in the flour, stir, and cook until the flour is combined but not brown. Slowly add the broth while whisking constantly. Add the salt, sliced shiitake caps and soaking liquid, the wild rice, and thyme. Bring to a boil over high heat, reduce the heat, and let simmer 10 minutes to allow flavors to blend.

½ cup boiling water

3 tablespoons sherry or rice wine

⅛-ounce package dried shiitake mushrooms

4 tablespoons (½ stick) unsalted butter

1 medium onion, diced (about 1 cup)

½ medium red or green bell pepper, cored, seeded, and finely diced (generous ⅓ cup)

1 celery rib, minced (about ⅔ cup)

3 ounces fresh mushrooms, sliced (about 1 cup)

2 tablespoons all-purpose flour

6 cups chicken broth

■ *3.* Season with the remaining table-spoon of sherry and the black pepper. Taste and adjust seasonings. Serve each bowl of soup topped with a mushroom slice.

½ teaspoon salt (omit if using canned broth)

1½ cups cooked wild rice (page 18)

½ teaspoon dried thyme leaves

Freshly ground black pepper to taste

6 thick mushroom slices, for garnish

# light minestra

*This is a quick, easy-to-make, and delicious soup.*

*4 servings*

- *1.* Heat the oil over high heat in a 4-quart saucepan, add the onion, and saute 2 minutes. Add the garlic and continue to saute an additional minute. Add the escarole and 1 cup broth, bring to a boil, cover, reduce the heat to medium, and cook for 10 minutes.
- *2.* Add the remaining broth and bring to a boil over high heat. Add the salt and rice, reduce the heat to low, cover, and cook for 15 to 20 minutes or until the rice is tender.
- *3.* Serve with lots of pepper and Parmesan cheese.

2 tablespoons olive oil

1 medium onion, chopped (about 1 cup)

3 garlic cloves, minced

1 head escarole, rinsed well and torn into bite-sized pieces

6 cups chicken broth

½ teaspoon salt (omit if using canned broth)

⅔ cup aromatic white rice or any rice blend that cooks in 15 to 20 minutes

Freshly ground black pepper

Freshly grated Parmesan cheese

# tomato rice bisque

*2 servings*

- *1.* Heat the oil in a 2-quart saucepan. Add the onion and saute until golden, about 5 minutes. Stir in the chili powder.
- *2.* Add 2 cups of the milk and bring to a boil. In a small bowl, gradually beat the remaining milk into the flour, then stir into the mixture in the saucepan along with the salt. Heat, while stirring, until the mixture boils and is thickened, about 5 minutes.
- *3.* Stir the tomato and rice into the milk mixture. Bring to a boil, remove from heat, and divide into serving dishes. Sprinkle with cilantro or parsley.

1 teaspoon rice bran oil or olive oil

½ small onion, finely chopped (about ¼ cup)

½ teaspoon chili powder

2½ cups milk

3 tablespoons all-purpose flour

1 teaspoon salt

1 large ripe tomato, peeled, seeded, and chopped (about 1¼ cups)

1 cup cooked white or brown rice (pages 14, 16)

1 tablespoon chopped fresh cilantro or parsley

# soupa
# avgolemono

*This lemon-infused soup is equally delicious when made with orzo, the rice-shaped pasta.*

*8 servings*

- *1.* Bring the broth and salt to a boil in a 4-quart saucepan over high heat; add the rice, stir, cover, reduce the heat, and simmer for 10 minutes, or until the rice is almost tender.
- *2.* In a small bowl, beat the eggs until frothy. Beat in the lemon juice, then add ½ cup of the simmering broth. Mix well.
- *3.* Slowly pour the egg mixture into the simmering broth, stirring constantly. Cook over low heat for 5 minutes or until the soup thickens enough to lightly coat a spoon. *Do not let the soup come to a boil* or the eggs will curdle.
- *4.* Taste and adjust seasonings. Serve immediately, sprinkled with parsley.

2 quarts chicken broth

1 teaspoon salt (omit if using canned broth)

⅔ cup U.S. Basmati rice

4 eggs

⅓ cup freshly squeezed lemon juice

Minced fresh parsley

# brown rice
# mexi-quiche

*6–8 servings as an appetizer*

■ *1.* Preheat the oven to 400°F. Generously grease a 10-inch pie pan.

■ *2.* Combine the rice, cheese, 2 eggs, salt, and pepper. Turn into the prepared pan, cover with wax paper or plastic wrap, and press firmly and evenly into the bottom and up the sides of the pan. Remove the wax paper or plastic wrap. Bake for 10 to 15 minutes, until the shell starts to color. Remove and cool on a rack.

■ *3.* Preheat the oven to 450°F. Sprinkle the chilies, pimiento, parsley, and jalapeño cheese into the cooled shell. Place the pie pan with the shell on a baking sheet. Mix together the remaining 2 eggs, half-and-half, cumin, salt, and pepper. Pour into the rice shell and bake for 15 minutes. Reduce the heat to 350°F. and bake for 30 minutes more, or until the filling is set. Let stand at least 15 minutes before serving.

3 cups cooked brown rice (page 16)

1 cup shredded Monterey Jack cheese (about 4 ounces)

4 eggs

Salt and freshly ground black pepper to taste

1 4-ounce can green chilies, diced

¼ cup diced pimiento

¼ cup chopped fresh parsley

1 cup shredded jalapeño Monterey Jack cheese (about 4 ounces)

1 cup half-and-half

½ teaspoon ground cumin

# winnie rice balls

*These crisp, chili-stuffed rice balls are a featured attraction at the annual Rice Festival in Winnie, Texas.*

*Makes 12 balls*

■ *1.* Heat the oil in a large skillet, saute the beef in the oil until browned. Add the celery, scallions, garlic, and chili powder. Cook until the vegetables are soft but not brown, about 5 minutes. Add the tomato sauce, salt, and pepper. Simmer for 15 minutes; stir in the parsley.

■ *2.* Meanwhile, combine the rice and 3½ cups water in a 3-quart saucepan. Bring to a boil over high heat; cover, reduce heat, and simmer for 20 minutes or until the water is absorbed and the rice is tender. Stir in the butter and Parmesan cheese. Cool just enough to handle.

■ *3.* Scoop about ⅓ cup of the cooked rice into one hand; flatten to ½ inch thickness. Spoon 2 to 3 tablespoons meat filling onto the center of the rice. Fold the rice mixture around the meat and roll into a ball. Repeat until

1 tablespoon rice bran oil or vegetable oil

¾ pound lean ground beef

1 celery rib, chopped (about ⅔ cup)

⅓ cup chopped scallions

1 garlic clove, minced

1 teaspoon chili powder

½ cup tomato sauce

Water

Salt and freshly ground black pepper to taste

1 tablespoon chopped fresh parsley

1½ cups short or medium grain white rice

4 tablespoons (½ stick) unsalted butter

¼ cup freshly grated Parmesan cheese

1 egg, beaten

2 cups toasted bread crumbs

Rice bran oil or vegetable oil for deep-fat frying

all the rice and meat have been used, making 12 balls.

■ 4. Heat 4 inches of oil in a 2-quart saucepan until it reaches 375°F. on a deep-fat thermometer. Dip the rice balls in the beaten egg and then in the crumbs. Fry in the hot fat until golden on all sides, about 5 minutes. Remove to paper towels to drain. Serve hot.

## Harvest Festivals

■

*Rice lovers can get more than a taste of their favorite grain at one of rice country's annual harvest festivals. In addition to duck calling competitions and fiddling at the International Rice Festival in Crowley, Louisiana, you can enjoy Southern rice specialties such as boudin, jambalaya, and gumbo.*

*Write to the local Chambers of Commerce for information on these festivals:*

*Harvest Rice Festival, Corning, Arkansas; last weekend in October.*

*International Rice Festival, Crowley, Louisiana; third weekend in October.*

*Katy Rice Festival, Katy, Texas; second weekend in October.*

*Texas Rice Festival, Winnie, Texas; first weekend in October.*

*Arkansas Rice Festival, Weiner, Arkansas; second weekend in October.*

# sushi

*The word* sushi *in Japanese refers to the rice flavored with seasoned vinegar that forms the basis of these tasty morsels, rather than to the raw fish as many Westerners think. This recipe makes one cucumber roll* (kappa maki), *one asparagus roll* (aspara maki), *and one avocado and crab roll (California roll). Sushi is best if prepared just before serving so the rice will be soft and creamy and the* nori *crisp.*

*Makes 3 rolls, 18 pieces*

■ *1.* In a 1-quart saucepan, combine the rice and water. Bring to a boil over high heat. Cover, reduce heat to low, and cook for 15 to 20 minutes, or until the rice is tender and the water is absorbed.

■ *2.* While the rice is cooking, prepare the fillings. Peel the cucumber and slice lengthwise into ¹⁄₁₆-inch-thick julienne strips. Wash, trim, and blanch the asparagus. Peel the avocado and slice lengthwise into ¼-inch-thick julienne strips; sprinkle with ½ teaspoon rice vinegar. Remove

¾ cup short grain white rice

1 cup water

½ small cucumber

3 thin stalks asparagus

¼ small avocado

Unseasoned rice vinegar or *sushi su* (seasoned rice vinegar)

1 cooked king crab leg

1 tablespoon sugar

½ teaspoon salt

3 7½ by 4-inch sheets *nori (laver)*

*Wasabi* (hot green horseradish; see note)

1 tablespoon toasted sesame seeds (see note page 103)

28

the crab meat from the shell and slice lengthwise.

■ *3.* Pour the cooked rice into a shallow baking dish. In the same saucepan, bring 2 tablespoons unseasoned vinegar, the sugar, and salt to a boil. (If using seasoned vinegar omit sugar and salt.) Pour over the rice. To give sushi rice its traditional glossy surface, it is important at this point to cool the rice quickly by cutting into it with a wooden rice paddle or spoon and tossing it lightly with the vinegar mixture while fanning with a cardboard fan or a piece of cardboard.

■ *4.* When the rice is cool, divide it into three portions. If *nori* is 7½ by 8, be sure to cut it in half. Toast one sheet of *nori* by holding it with tongs and moving it back and forth above direct heat (flame or electric coil) until it changes to a brighter green color and releases a sea-like fragrance. Turn and toast on the other side. Place the toasted *nori* at one end of the bamboo rolling mat with 7½-inch edge toward you. With moistened fingers, spread one third of the sushi rice over about three fourths of the *nori,* being careful to spread it to the edges.

*Amazu shoga* (pink pickled ginger; see note)

Soy sauce

Special equipment: bamboo rolling mat (see note)

Place the cucumber strips lengthwise in the center of the rice. If desired, spread with a little *wasabi*.

■ *5.* Using the bamboo mat to hold the ingredients, lift the rice-covered end of the *nori* and roll up toward the uncovered end. Being careful to keep the bamboo mat on the outside of the roll, press firmly and roll back and forth several times. Remove the cucumber roll to a cutting board. Repeat with the asparagus to make the asparagus roll.

■ *6.* To make the California roll, start at one end and sprinkle toasted sesame seeds over three quarters of the bamboo rolling mat. Spread the remaining rice on the mat over the sesame seeds to form a rectangle the size of the remaining *nori.* Toast the *nori* and place on the rice. On the end of the *nori* that is at the end of the mat, arrange the avocado and crab. Start rolling from the avocado and crab and, using the mat to hold the ingredients, roll firmly until all the rice has been incorporated. Being careful to keep the bamboo mat on the outside of the roll, press firmly and roll back and forth several times. Remove the California roll to a cutting board.

■ 7. Trim the ends of the rolls with a moist, sharp knife. Cut each roll into thirds. Moisten the knife again and cut each third in half diagonally. Set the pieces of sushi on the serving plate with the level ends down. Serve with *wasabi, amazu shoga,* and soy sauce.

**Note:** *Wasabi* is available powdered, to be reconstituted, or in tubes of paste. *Amazu shoga* comes in jars or vacuum packs. Both, as well as *nori,* rice vinegar, and bamboo rolling mats, are available in Japanese food stores and some supermarkets and gourmet shops.

## RICE THROWING AND FERTILITY

*The custom of throwing rice at the bride and groom can be traced back to the Roman wedding tradition of holding sheaves of wheat during the ceremony. No one really knows when the grain changed to rice, but it has been suggested that when the wheat became wedding cake, people threw rice because it was white and not expensive. Whatever the reason, throwing seeds of grain is clearly a message to the couple to "go forth and multiply."*

# stuffed shiitake mushrooms

*6–8 servings*

- *1.* Clean the mushrooms; discard the stems if using shiitake mushrooms. Reserve regular mushroom stems for another purpose. Heat the olive oil and butter in a medium skillet. Saute the mushrooms until golden on both sides; remove to a bowl. Add the onion, green pepper, and basil to skillet; saute, stirring, until the onion is golden, about 5 minutes. Stir in the rice, cream cheese, salt, and pepper.
- *2.* Preheat the oven to 350°F. Arrange the mushrooms, rib side up, on a rimmed cookie sheet. Divide the rice mixture among the mushrooms. Bake just until the mushrooms are reheated, about 10 minutes. Top each with a parsley sprig, if desired, and serve.
- *3.* The mushrooms can be assembled (without parsley sprigs) and refrigerated, covered, for several hours or overnight, then reheated in a 350°F oven for 20 minutes until hot.

¾ pound fresh shiitake or regular mushrooms (about 24 medium)

1 teaspoon olive oil

1 teaspoon unsalted butter

½ small red onion, finely chopped (about ¼ cup)

½ medium green pepper, cored, seeded, and finely chopped (generous ⅓ cup)

½ teaspoon dried basil

¾ cup cooked brown rice or white rice (see pages 16, 14)

2 tablespoons cream cheese

Salt and freshly ground black pepper to taste

24 sprigs fresh parsley (optional)

# wild rice pancakes with caviar

*An easy-to-make show stopper. If your budget allows, double the caviar and use two colors.*

*6 servings*

■ *1.* Stir the flour, baking powder, dillweed, pepper, and salt together in a small bowl. Add the egg, milk, and 1 tablespoon oil. Stir until the flour is moistened. The batter will be lumpy. Fold in the wild rice and parsley.

■ *2.* Heat 1 teaspoon oil in a large skillet. Drop the pancake batter into the skillet, 1 level tablespoon at a time, to make 18 to 20 pancakes about 2½ inches in diameter. Fry until golden on one side; turn and fry until golden on the other, about 3 to 5 minutes in all. Continue cooking the pancakes until all the batter is used. Keep the pancakes warm in a 250°F. oven while frying the others.

■ *3.* To serve, divide the pancakes onto individual serving plates. Top each pancake with a dollop of sour cream and some caviar.

⅔ cup all-purpose flour

1 teaspoon baking powder

¼ teaspoon dried dill weed

¼ teaspoon cracked black pepper

⅛ teaspoon salt

1 egg, lightly beaten

½ cup milk

Vegetable oil

½ cup cooked wild rice (page 18)

1 tablespoon chopped fresh parsley

1 cup sour cream

2 ounces caviar

# saffron rice timbales

*4 servings*

- *1.* Heat 1 teaspoon oil in a heavy 2-quart saucepan. Add the onion and mushrooms and saute until golden, 3 to 5 minutes. Stir in the rice, water, salt, and saffron. Bring to a boil over high heat; reduce the heat, cover, and cook about 18 to 20 minutes or until the rice is tender and the liquid is absorbed.
- *2.* Meanwhile, preheat the broiler. Cut the peppers in half; discard the seeds and membranes. Arrange the peppers on a broiler pan, cut side down, and brush them with oil. Broil 4 inches from the heat until the skins are blackened, about 4 or 5 minutes. Place the peppers on a large piece of aluminum foil. Wrap tightly and set aside for 5 minutes to allow the steam to loosen the pepper skins.
- *3.* Preheat the oven to 350°F. Generously oil four 6-ounce timbale molds or custard cups.
- *4.* Stir the carrot and zucchini into the rice mixture. Divide the rice mix-

Olive oil

½ small onion, finely chopped (about ¼ cup)

2 medium mushrooms, finely chopped

¾ cup short or medium grain white rice

1¾ cups water

½ teaspoon salt

¼ teaspoon saffron threads

3 medium bell peppers (1 each red, yellow, and green)

½ carrot, shredded

½ small zucchini, shredded

ture among the molds and press it firmly with the back of a spoon. Cover and bake for 15 minutes.

■ 5. Peel the skin from the peppers; cut each pepper half into 4 strips. Rewrap in the aluminum foil and reheat in the oven for the last 5 minutes of the timbale baking time.

■ 6. To serve, invert the timbales onto individual serving plates. Arrange the peppers around the timbales. Serve immediately.

*Sweet or glutinous rice is an opaque, short grain rice used in many traditional Japanese dishes. To prepare it you must soak it for at least 12 hours in water to cover; drain it and steam it in a thin layer for 20 to 25 minutes or until it is tender.*

# salads

"Same old slippers,

Same old rice,

Same old glimpse of

Paradise."

William James

Lampton,

June Weddings

# sesame rice salad

*4–6 servings*

■ *1.* Bring the water to a boil in a 2-quart saucepan over high heat. Add the rice, garlic, and salt; stir, cover, reduce the heat, and cook for 15 to 20 minutes or until the liquid is absorbed and the rice is tender. Remove from the heat and let stand, covered, for 5 minutes.

■ *2.* To prepare the dressing, mix the vegetable oil, sesame oil, rice vinegar, soy sauce, and ginger in a small bowl. Toss together in a small bowl the peas, onion, water chestnuts, and red pepper, then add to the warm rice along with the dressing and the sesame seeds, if desired. Toss thoroughly, taste, and adjust seasonings. Serve lukewarm or refrigerate until 30 minutes before serving.

Note: To substitute brown or a blended rice, adjust the amount of liquid used and the cooking time according to the package directions.

2 cups water

1 cup white rice (see note)

1 garlic clove, minced

¼ teaspoon salt

2 tablespoons vegetable oil

2 tablespoons Oriental sesame oil

2 tablespoons rice vinegar

1 teaspoon soy sauce

½ teaspoon minced fresh ginger

¾ cup fresh snow peas or sugar snap peas, blanched

½ medium red onion, minced (about ½ cup)

12 water chestnuts, cubed

1 medium red bell pepper, cored, seeded, and diced (about ¾ cup)

1 tablespoon toasted sesame seeds (optional)

# greek-style rice salad

*This is a delicious accompaniment to barbecued lamb or lemon-marinated chicken, or as a light luncheon entree with some crusty bread.*

*4–6 servings*

■ *1.* Bring the water to a boil in a 2-quart saucepan over high heat. Add the rice, stir, cover, reduce the heat, and cook for 15 to 20 minutes or until all the liquid is absorbed and the rice is tender. Remove from the heat and let stand, covered, for 5 minutes.

■ *2.* To prepare the marinade, in a medium bowl whisk together the oil, lemon juice, oregano, mustard, salt, and pepper. Mix in the tomatoes, feta, olives, and parsley and allow to marinate while the rice is cooking.

■ *3.* Place the hot rice in a large serving bowl. Drain the marinade over the hot rice, toss, and let cool slightly. Add the tomato-feta mixture and toss. Taste and adjust seasonings. Serve lukewarm or refrigerate until 30 minutes before serving.

2 cups water

1 cup white rice (see note)

6 tablespoons olive oil

2 tablespoons freshly squeezed lemon juice

1 teaspoon dried oregano leaves

½ teaspoon Dijon mustard

Pinch salt

Freshly ground black pepper to taste

2 large ripe tomatoes, peeled, seeded, and diced (about 2 cups)

½ pound feta cheese, crumbled

¾ cup sliced pitted black olives, preferably imported

¼ cup chopped fresh parsley

**Note:** To substitute brown or a blended rice, adjust the amount of liquid used and the cooking time according to the package directions.

## Molded Rice Salads

■

*For molded rice salads, pack any of these salads into a well-greased mold, press down firmly, cover with wax paper, and weigh for 30 minutes, using cans or other weights, before unmolding onto a serving platter. A ring mold makes an attractive presentation, especially when the center is overflowing with one of the salad ingredients. For instance, fill a ring of Greek-Style Rice Salad with chopped tomatoes, feta cheese, or olives.*

# wild rice, sun-dried tomatoes, and smoked turkey salad

*This is a fabulous combination, perfect for picnics or parties.*

*4–6 servings*

■ *1.* Rinse the wild rice under running water. Bring the water to a boil in a 2-quart saucepan over high heat. Add the rice, stir, reduce the heat, cover, and cook for 45 to 50 minutes, or until the rice is tender. Drain off any excess liquid.

■ *2.* While the rice is cooking, pour boiling water to cover over the sun-dried tomatoes and let stand 10 to 20 minutes, until soft. Drain and cut into thin strips.

■ *3.* In a large bowl, combine the tomatoes with the turkey, cucumber, scallions, oil, vinegar, salt, and pepper. Add to the warm rice and toss. Taste and adjust seasonings. Serve on lettuce-lined plates, lukewarm, or refrigerate until 30 minutes before serving.

¾ cups wild rice

2¼ cups water

12 sun-dried tomatoes (see note)

½ pound smoked turkey, cut into ½-inch cubes

1 cucumber, peeled, seeded, and cut into ½-inch cubes (about 1 cup)

½ cup minced scallions

¼ cup olive oil

2 tablespoons red wine vinegar

Salt and freshly ground black pepper to taste

Red leaf lettuce

**Note:** Sun-dried tomatoes can be purchased either packed in olive oil or dried. It is more economical to purchase them dried and reconstitute them, as done in this recipe.

## Edible Bowls

∎

*For an unusual brunch presentation, fill hollowed-out tomato halves with any of these rice salads. Precooked zucchini, Jack-be-Little pumpkin, pattypan squash, or a mixture of red, green, and yellow bell peppers work just as well. Either cut the zucchini or bell peppers in half lengthwise for a boatlike presentation or remove the seeds from the pumpkin, squash, or pepper and fill with the rice.*

*As an accompaniment to a roast, stuff a tomato, zucchini, or pepper half with rice pilaf or another favorite rice side dish and, if desired, bake at 350°F. until heated through.*

# curried rice salad

*6–8 servings*

- *1.* Bring the broth to a boil in a 2-quart saucepan over high heat. Add the rice and salt, stir, lower the heat, cover, and cook for 45 minutes, or until the rice is tender. Remove from the heat and toss with the sesame oil.
- *2.* In a large bowl, combine the carrot, scallions, curry, cumin, garlic, pine nuts, lime juice, vinegar, soy, parsley, chutney, and raisins. Mix well. Add the warm rice to the bowl and toss to mix.
- *3.* Taste and adjust seasonings. Serve lukewarm or refrigerate until 30 minutes before serving.

3 cups chicken broth

1½ cups brown rice

¾ teaspoon salt (omit if using canned broth)

1 tablespoon Oriental sesame oil

½ cup julienne strips carrot

4 scallions, white part only, minced

2 teaspoons hot curry powder, or to taste

¼ teaspoon ground cumin

1 garlic clove, minced

2 tablespoons toasted pine nuts (pignoli)

2 tablespoons freshly squeezed lime juice

1 tablespoon rice wine vinegar

2 tablespoons soy sauce

1 tablespoon minced fresh parsley

3 tablespoons mango chutney, chopped

½ cup raisins

# confetti rice salad

*6–8 servings*

■ *1.* Bring the water to a boil in a 2-quart saucepan over high heat. Add the rice, salt, bay leaf, and lemon juice; stir, cover, reduce the heat, and cook for 15 to 20 minutes or until the liquid is absorbed and the rice is tender. Remove from the heat and let stand, covered, for 5 minutes.

■ *2.* To prepare the dressing, whisk together in a small bowl the oil, vinegar, mustard, garlic, and pepper. In a large bowl, combine the peas, tomatoes, scallions, parsley, and basil and add the warm rice along with the dressing. Toss thoroughly. Taste and adjust seasonings. Serve lukewarm or refrigerate until 30 minutes before serving.

Note: To substitute brown or a blended rice, adjust the amount of liquid used and the cooking time according to the package directions.

2 cups water

1 cup white rice (see note)

1 teaspoon salt

1 bay leaf

1 teaspoon freshly squeezed lemon juice

½ cup vegetable oil

3 tablespoons red wine vinegar

½ teaspoon dry mustard

1 garlic clove, minced

Freshly ground black pepper to taste

1 cup frozen green peas

2 medium tomatoes, peeled, seeded, and diced (about 1½ cups)

⅓ cup minced scallions (about 2 medium)

¼ cup chopped fresh parsley

1 tablespoon dried basil

# rice salad niçoise

*A rice version of a salad classic*

*6–8 servings*

■ *1.* To prepare the dressing, whisk together in a large bowl the oil, vinegar, lemon juice, garlic, oregano, salt, and pepper to taste. Add the onion, artichokes, olives, and tuna. Toss and let marinate while preparing the rice.

■ *2.* Bring the broth to a boil in a 2-quart saucepan over high heat. Add the rice, stir, reduce the heat, cover, and cook for 15 to 20 minutes, or until all the liquid is absorbed and the rice is tender. Remove from the heat and let stand, covered, 5 minutes, then toss with the marinated mixture.

■ *3.* Taste and adjust seasonings. Serve lukewarm or refrigerate until 30 minutes before serving. Garnish with green beans, egg slices, and tomatoes. Toss well before serving.

**Note:** To substitute brown or a blended rice, adjust the amount of liquid used and the cooking time according to the package directions.

1 cup olive oil

⅓ cup red wine vinegar

2 tablespoons freshly squeezed lemon juice

2 garlic cloves, minced

1 teaspoon dried oregano leaves

¼ teaspoon salt

Freshly ground black pepper

1 medium onion, minced (about 1 cup)

1 8-ounce can artichoke hearts in water, drained and quartered

1 cup black olives, sliced

2 7½-ounce cans white tuna, drained

4 cups chicken broth

2 cups white rice (see note)

1 pound green beans, trimmed, blanched, and cut into 2-inch pieces

4 hard-cooked eggs

Tomato wedges

# paella salad

*This is a cold version of the hot Spanish classic.*

*6 servings*

■ *1.* In a large bowl, whisk together the oil, vinegar, parsley, lemon juice, garlic, salt, and pepper to taste. Add the red pepper, chicken, shrimp, sausage, scallions, and tomato. Let marinate while preparing rice.

■ *2.* Bring the broth to a boil in a 2-quart saucepan over high heat. Add the rice and saffron. Stir, cover, reduce the heat, and cook for 15 to 20 minutes, or until all the liquid is absorbed and the rice is tender. Remove from the heat and let stand, covered, for 5 minutes. Add to the marinated mixture and toss.

■ *3.* Taste and adjust seasonings. Serve lukewarm or refrigerate until 30 minutes before serving. Garnish with peas. Toss well before serving.

Note: To substitute brown or a blended rice, adjust the amount of liquid used and the cooking time according to the package directions.

½ cup olive oil

3 tablespoons red wine vinegar

2 tablespoons chopped fresh parsley

1 tablespoon freshly squeezed lemon juice

1 garlic clove, minced

¼ teaspoon salt

Freshly ground black pepper

1 medium red bell pepper, cored, seeded, and cut into julienne strips (about ¾ cup)

1½ cups cubed, cooked chicken

½ pound cooked shrimp

½ pound hot sausage (chorizo preferred), cooked and cut into chunks

2 scallions, including 2 inches green tops, minced

1 large tomato, peeled, seeded, and diced (about 1¼ cups)

2 cups chicken broth

1 cup white rice (see note)

¼ teaspoon saffron threads

1 cup frozen peas, thawed

# one-dish meals

Rice . . . is a flavor extender— it makes more costly foods go farther.

Rice—200 Delightful Ways To Serve It, *The Southern Rice Industry,* 1936

# chicken and crab pilau

*6 servings*

■ *1.* Saute the celery and onion in the butter in a 4-quart Dutch oven. Add the chicken and saute until lightly browned, about 10 minutes.

■ *2.* Stir in the rice, then add the water, tomatoes, salt, pepper, and Tabasco. Bring to a boil; cover tightly and cook over low heat for 45 minutes, stirring occasionally, until the rice is tender and most of the liquid is absorbed.

■ *3.* Stir in the crab and crab-boil seasoning, if desired. Cook over very low heat for 5 to 10 minutes or until the crab is heated through. Turn out onto a large platter or serve from the Dutch oven.

**Note:** There are many good regional crab-boil or seafood seasonings. We use *Old Bay Seasoning,* which is produced by the Baltimore Spice Company. You may use your favorite or omit the seasoning for a milder flavor.

1 celery rib, sliced (about ⅔ cup)

1 small onion, chopped (about ½ cup)

1 teaspoon unsalted butter or olive oil

2 whole chicken breasts, skinned and boned and cut into 1-inch pieces (about 1 pound)

¾ cup brown rice

1½ cups water

2 large ripe fresh tomatoes, peeled and coarsely chopped (about 2½ cups)

¾ teaspoon salt

¼ teaspoon cracked black pepper

2 or 3 drops Tabasco

½ pound fresh crab meat

½ teaspoon crab-boil seasoning (optional; see note)

# andouille jambalaya

*There are as many recipes for jambalaya in the South as there are cooks. Some add duck, chicken, sausage, shrimp, and/or other seafood. Vary this recipe to your liking; it is hot and spicy.*

*4–6 servings*

■ *1.* Heat the oil in a heavy-bottomed 2-quart saucepan over medium heat. Add 1½ cups onions and cook, uncovered, stirring occasionally, until the onions are caramelized but do not burn, about 5 to 10 minutes.

■ *2.* Add the remaining onions, the sausage, green pepper, celery, and garlic. Cook, stirring frequently, for 5 minutes. Add the rice and stir to coat with oil. Add the tomatoes, oregano, Tabasco, thyme, cayenne, bay leaf, and chicken broth. Bring to a boil over high heat, cover, reduce the heat, and cook until the liquid is absorbed and rice is tender, about 25 minutes.

2 tablespoons vegetable oil

2 large onions, chopped (about 3 cups)

¾ pound andouille or other smoked pork sausage, thinly sliced

1 medium green bell pepper, cored, seeded, and coarsely chopped (about ¾ cup)

1 celery rib, chopped (about ⅔ cup)

2 garlic cloves, minced

1 cup long grain white rice

1 14½-ounce can crushed tomatoes in puree (about 2 cups)

2 teaspoons dried oregano leaves

1 teaspoon Tabasco

½ teaspoon dried thyme leaves

½ teaspoon cayenne (ground red) pepper

1 bay leaf

2 cups chicken broth

1 pound medium shrimp, peeled and deveined

■ *3.* Add the shrimp, cover, and cook an additional 5 minutes over low heat, or until the shrimp are pink. Taste and adjust seasoning.

*"Jambalaya,*

*crawfish pie,*

*file gumbo*

*Son of a gun, have*

*great fun on*

*the bayou."*

"Jambalaya,"

*popularized by*

*Hank Williams*

# shrimp creole

*In old New Orleans, Creole cooks served a spicy tomato sauce over rice. This one-dish meal is an all-American version of that classic.*

*4–6 servings*

■ *1.* Heat the oil in a heavy saucepan over medium-high heat. Add the onion, bell pepper, celery, and garlic, and saute until the onion is translucent, about 5 minutes. Add the tomatoes, broth, bay leaf, cayenne, paprika, salt, and pepper. Bring to a boil over high heat. Add the rice, stir, reduce the heat, cover, and cook for 20 to 30 minutes, until the rice is tender.

■ *2.* Add the shrimp, cover, and cook until the shrimp are pink and firm to the touch, about 5 minutes. Remove the bay leaf, taste and adjust seasonings, and serve.

**Variation:** Omit the uncooked rice and broth. Simmer the seasoned tomatoes 20 minutes before adding shrimp. Serve over cooked rice.

3 tablespoons vegetable oil

1 medium onion, coarsely chopped (about 1 cup)

1 medium green bell pepper, cored, seeded, and coarsely chopped (about ¾ cup)

2 celery ribs, coarsely chopped (about 1⅓ cups)

1 garlic clove, minced

4 cups peeled, seeded, and diced tomatoes (about 4 large) *or* 1 28-ounce can crushed tomatoes

2½ cups chicken broth or water

1 bay leaf

¼ teaspoon cayenne (ground red) pepper

½ teaspoon sweet paprika

Salt and freshly ground black pepper to taste

1 cup U.S. aromatic rice

2 pounds medium shrimp, peeled and deveined

# chicken gumbo

*Make this with fresh chicken, or use leftover chunks of cooked chicken and add it along with okra.*

*4–6 servings*

■ *1.* Heat the oil in a heavy-bottomed 4-quart saucepan over high heat. To make a roux, stir in the flour, reduce the heat, and cook over medium heat for about 15 minutes, stirring occasionally, until a dark caramel color. Do not burn the roux or it will be bitter.

■ *2.* Add the onion and cook, while stirring, until wilted, about 5 minutes. Add the green pepper, celery, scallions, and garlic and continue stirring a few minutes longer.

■ *3.* Add the undrained tomatoes, broth, chicken, bay leaf, hot pepper, salt, and black pepper. Bring to a boil over high heat, add the rice, stir, reduce the heat, cover, and let simmer 35 minutes. Add the okra and corn, return to a simmer, cover, and cook 10 minutes more, until the rice is tender. Taste and adjust seasonings.

⅓ cup vegetable oil

⅓ cup all-purpose flour

1 medium onion, coarsely chopped (about 1 cup)

1 medium green bell pepper, seeded, cored, and chopped (about ¾ cup)

2 celery ribs, diced (about 1⅓ cups)

½ cup minced scallions

2 garlic cloves, minced

1 14½-ounce can plum tomatoes

3½ cups chicken broth

1 chicken, about 3 pounds, cut into eighths, skinned

1 bay leaf

½ teaspoon hot pepper flakes

Salt and freshly ground black pepper to taste

1 cup brown rice

1 10-ounce package frozen cut okra

1½ cups fresh or frozen corn

# lamb couscous

*4 servings*

■ *1.* Heat the oil in the bottom of a large couscousiere or large, heavy-bottomed steamer. Add the lamb shanks and saute until browned on all sides, about 8 to 10 minutes. Add the onion and cook while stirring until lightly browned, about 3 minutes.

■ *2.* Finely chop 1 carrot half, 1 turnip half, and 1 zucchini half. Slice the remaining vegetables ¼ inch thick; wrap the sliced vegetables and refrigerate.

■ *3.* Stir the chopped vegetables into the onion in the pan along with the tomatoes, 1 ½ cups water, ¼ teaspoon salt, the pepper, saffron, and cinnamon. Bring to a boil over high heat; reduce heat to low, cover, and simmer until the lamb is tender, about 1¼ to 1½ hours, adding more water, if necessary, to keep from burning.

■ *4.* When the lamb is tender, prepare the couscous in salted water according to the package directions.

■ *5.* While the couscous is cooking, remove the lamb from the saucepan. Skim the fat from the broth and veg-

1 tablespoon rice bran oil or olive oil

2 medium lamb shanks (about 2 pounds)

1 small onion, chopped (about ½ cup)

2 carrots, peeled and halved crosswise

2 medium turnips, peeled and halved

2 medium zucchini, halved crosswise

1 14¼-ounce can stewed tomatoes

Water

Salt

¼ teaspoon cracked black pepper

¼ teaspoon saffron threads

¼ teaspoon ground cinnamon

¾ cup rice couscous (see mail order sources, page 127)

½ cup milk

etable mixture and discard. Place the broth and vegetable mixture in a blender and blend until smooth. If necessary add water to make 2½ cups of sauce. Remove the lamb from the ̣ones.

■ 6. Return the vegetable sauce and lamb pieces to the bottom of the couscousiere or steamer. Stir in the reserved sliced carrots and turnips. Fluff the couscous with a fork. Stir the milk into the couscous. Place the couscous in the top of the couscousiere or in the steamer basket (it should be at least 1 inch above the stew).

■ 7. Bring the lamb stew to a boil over low heat and simmer 10 minutes. Fold the zucchini slices into the stew and cook, with couscous still on top, for 10 minutes longer or until carrots and turnips are tender.

■ 8. To serve, fluff the couscous with a fork and spread it out on a serving platter. Spoon the lamb stew on top of the couscous and serve.

## A Roux Awakening

■

*A roux is a mixture of a starch, usually flour, and a fat, often butter, cooked together until thickened. In the South, a roux is cooked until the mixture is brown in color. This golden or brown roux (depending on how long the mixture is cooked) is the thickening agent for many soups, stews, and sauces.*

*To make a roux, cook equal amounts of starch and fat, while stirring, until the desired color is achieved (10 minutes to one hour on the stovetop; 7 to 8 minutes in the microwave). To make a roux in the microwave, combine the flour and fat in a glass measuring cup. Microwave on high (100 percent) for 4 minutes, remove from the oven, and stir. Microwave for 1 minute on high (100 percent) and stir. Repeat two or three more times, until the roux is the desired color.*

# red beans and rice

*In Louisiana, folks traditionally served red beans and rice on Mondays. They cooked the beans, along with the leftover ham bone from Sunday's dinner, all day while the wash was done, and used the rice water to starch the clothes.*

*4–6 servings*

■ *1.* Cover the beans with water in a 4-quart saucepan, bring to a boil, and cook for 2 minutes. Remove the beans from the heat, and allow to stand partially covered for 1 hour. Drain the water from the beans.

■ *2.* Return the beans to the pot. Add 5 cups water, the onions, celery, garlic, ham hocks, Tabasco, black pepper, and cayenne. Bring to a boil over high heat, reduce the heat, and simmer, partially covered, for about 3 hours or until the beans are tender.

■ *3.* Remove the ham hocks. When cool enough to handle, trim the meat from the bone and chop; discard the bone and fat. Stir the meat into the beans, mash some of the beans against

1 pound red or kidney beans, picked over and rinsed

Water

2 medium onions, chopped (about 2 cups)

2 celery ribs, chopped (about 1 ⅓ cups)

2 garlic cloves, minced

2 pounds smoked ham hocks

1 teaspoon Tabasco

½ teaspoon freshly ground black pepper

½ teaspoon cayenne (ground red) pepper

3 cups cooked brown or white rice (pages 16, 14)

Sliced andouille or other smoked pork sausage, cooked (optional)

the side of the pan, and stir until the mixture is thickened. The beans should be stewlike. If not, continue cooking, uncovered, over medium heat to thicken. Taste and adjust seasoning. Serve over hot rice with, if desired, sliced andouille or other smoked pork sausage.

*Louis Armstrong*

*signed his letters:*

*"Red beans and*

*ricely yours."*

# quick paella

*For an even quicker version, buy cooked shrimp and tuck them into the rice 10 minutes before the paella is done.*

*6 servings*

- *1.* Preheat the oven to 350°F.
- *2.* In a 4-quart ovenproof casserole or paella pan, cook the sausage over medium heat until cooked through. Remove and set aside sausage, reserving 2 tablespoons of the drippings in the skillet. Add the onion, green and red peppers, and garlic and cook about 5 minutes, until the onion is tender.
- *3.* Add the rice and stir until it is translucent and faintly golden, about 3 minutes. Add the tomatoes, saffron, water, and salt; bring to a boil and remove from heat. Stir in the reserved sausage, the shrimp, clams, and peas.

1 pound *chorizo* or other garlic sausage, sliced

1 medium onion, chopped (about 1 cup)

1 medium green bell pepper, cored, seeded, and sliced (about ¾ cup)

1 medium red bell pepper, cored, seeded, and sliced (about ¾ cup)

4 garlic cloves, minced

2 cups long grain parboiled white rice

1 cup drained and chopped canned tomatoes

½ teaspoon crushed saffron threads (¼ teaspoon turmeric can be substituted, but the taste will not be the same)

1 quart water or chicken broth

1 teaspoon salt (omit if using canned broth)

■ *4.* Cover the casserole and bake in the preheated oven for 30 to 35 minutes, until the rice is tender, the liquid is absorbed, and the shrimp is cooked. Discard any clams that do not open. Garnish with lemon slices.

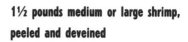

**1½ pounds medium or large shrimp, peeled and deveined**

**12 hardshell clams in shell, thoroughly scrubbed**

**1 10-ounce package frozen peas**

**Sliced lemon, for garnish**

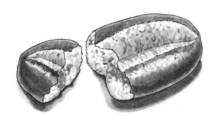

# elaborate paella

*Saffron provides the bright yellow color and classic taste.*

*6–8 servings*

- *1.* Preheat the oven to 350°F.
- *2.* Season the chicken with salt and pepper. Heat the olive oil in a 4-quart skillet or saucepan and brown the chicken on all sides. Remove the chicken and set aside. In the same skillet brown the sausage, remove, and set aside.
- *3.* Add the garlic and onion to the skillet, and saute until the onion is soft, about 5 minutes. Add the rice and cook until translucent and lightly golden, about 3 minutes. Add the tomatoes, capers, saffron, broth, salt, and pepper, then stir to loosen any browned bits at bottom of pan. Bring to a boil over high heat, add the reserved chicken and sausage, cover, reduce heat, and simmer for 15 minutes.
- *4.* Transfer the mixture to a very large ovenproof casserole or paella pan. Tuck the lobster, shrimp, mussels, and clams into the rice. Arrange the pimiento and peas on top. Cover

1 chicken, about 3 pounds, cut into serving pieces

Salt and freshly ground black pepper to taste

Olive oil

1 pound *chorizo* or other garlic sausage, sliced

1 garlic clove, minced

1 medium onion, chopped (about 1 cup)

2 cups long grain white rice

3 large tomatoes, peeled, seeded, and chopped, *or* 3 cups drained and chopped canned tomatoes

1 tablespoon capers, rinsed and drained

½ teaspoon crushed saffron threads (¼ teaspoon turmeric can be substituted but the taste will not be the same)

and bake in the preheated oven for 15 to 20 minutes or until the clams and mussels open and the shrimp and lobster are cooked. If the paella looks dry, add ¼ cup additional broth or water, but do not stir.

■ 5. Remove the paella from the oven and let stand, covered, for 5 minutes. Discard any clams or mussels that are not open. Garnish with lemon slices and serve.

**1 quart chicken broth**

**2-pound lobster cut into pieces (have fishmonger cut a live lobster into pieces)**

**12 large shrimp, peeled and deveined, tails left on**

**12 mussels, debearded, thoroughly scrubbed, and well rinsed**

**12 hardshell clams in shell, thoroughly scrubbed and well rinsed**

**1 4-ounce jar pimientos, cut into strips**

**1 cup frozen peas**

**Sliced lemon, for garnish**

# chili

*Here's a chili that can be made in less than an hour. For an even faster version, use white rice and reduce the cooking time to 25 minutes after adding the rice.*

*6 servings*

■ *1.* Heat the oil in a 4-quart saucepan over medium-high heat. Add the onion and peppers, then saute until soft, about 5 minutes. Add the beef and cook just until it loses its pink color.

■ *2.* Stir in the chili, cumin, oregano, and cayenne. Add the tomato puree, 2 cups water, and the kidney beans, and simmer for 5 minutes.

■ *3.* Add remaining 2 cups water and bring to a boil over high heat. Stir in the rice, reduce the heat, cover, and simmer for 40 to 45 minutes, until the rice is tender.

■ *4.* Remove from heat and let stand 5 minutes before serving.

2 tablespoons vegetable or rice bran oil

1 medium onion, minced (about 1 cup)

1 medium green or red bell pepper, cored, seeded, and minced (about ¾ cup)

2 jalapeño peppers, seeded and minced

1½ pounds lean ground beef

2 to 3 tablespoons chili powder

1 teaspoon ground cumin

½ teaspoon dried oregano leaves

Pinch cayenne (ground red) pepper

1 15-ounce can tomato puree (about 2 cups)

4 cups water

1 15½-ounce can kidney beans, drained

1 cup brown rice

Salt and freshly ground black pepper to taste

# lisa dishman's casserole

*When we asked rice farmer Bill Dish-man of China, Texas, what his favorite rice dish was, he told us his daughter-in-law, Lisa, made this wonderful casserole. Lisa told us that she adapted the recipe from one in their church's cookbook.*

*6 servings*

■ *1.* Preheat the oven to 350°F. Lightly grease a 13 by 9 by 2–inch baking dish.

■ *2.* In a large bowl, toss together the rice, crawfish, crab, celery, onion, and green pepper. Stir the mayonnaise, curry powder, cayenne, and salt into the rice mixture. Spoon into the greased baking dish. Sprinkle paprika over the top.

■ *3.* Bake the casserole for 1 hour, or until golden brown on top and bubbly in the center. Serve immediately.

3 cups cooked long grain white rice (page 14)

2 pounds crawfish tails or cleaned, deveined shrimp

1 pound crab meat

½ celery rib, finely chopped (about ⅓ cup)

1 small onion, finely chopped (about ½ cup)

½ medium green bell pepper, cored, seeded, and finely chopped (generous ⅓ cup)

¾ cup mayonnaise

1 teaspoon curry powder

1 teaspoon cayenne (ground red) pepper

½ teaspoon salt

¼ teaspoon paprika

# arroz con pollo

*Chicken with rice is one of the classic dishes of Spain.*

*4–6 servings*

■ *1.* Season the chicken with salt and pepper. Heat the oil in a large skillet. Brown the chicken in the oil, remove to a platter, and set aside. Pour off all but about 2 tablespoons oil from the skillet. Add the onion, bell pepper, and garlic and saute until the onion is translucent, about 5 minutes.

■ *2.* Add the bay leaf, tomatoes, coriander, ham, and broth and bring to a boil over high heat. Stir in the rice, saffron, and chicken; reduce the heat, cover, and cook until the chicken is tender, about 30 minutes.

■ *3.* Add the peas and pimiento, cover, and cook 5 additional minutes. Taste and adjust seasonings.

**Variation**: Spanish Chicken and Rice. For a slightly different version, double the amount of onions, use a

1 frying chicken, 3 to 3½ pounds, cut into eighths

Salt and freshly ground black pepper to taste

2 tablespoons vegetable oil

1 medium onion, finely chopped (about 1 cup)

1 medium green bell pepper, cored, seeded, and finely chopped (about ¾ cup)

2 garlic cloves, minced

1 bay leaf

2 medium tomatoes, peeled, seeded, and diced (about 1½ cups)

2 tablespoons chopped fresh coriander or parsley

1 cup finely diced cooked ham

red bell pepper instead of the green, and drain and quarter one 14-ounce can of artichoke hearts in water; add onions, peppers, and artichokes to the pan. Add ⅛ teaspoon saffron when adding the rice and omit the pimiento.

**3 cups chicken broth or water**

**1½ cups long grain white rice**

**½ teaspoon saffron**

**1 cup frozen peas *or* 1 cup blanched fresh peas**

**½ cup diced pimiento**

# chicken with rice dumplings

*4 servings*

■ *1.* Heat 1 tablespoon oil in a heavy, 4-quart Dutch oven. Add the chicken pieces and saute until golden on all sides, about 10 minutes. Remove chicken to a plate. Add the onion, celery, and mushrooms to the Dutch oven. Saute, stirring, until the onion is golden, about 5 minutes. Return chicken to Dutch oven.

■ *2.* Gradually stir in the water. Add ½ teaspoon salt and the thyme. Bring to a boil over high heat, reduce heat to low, cover, and cook until the chicken is almost tender, about 35 minutes.

■ *3.* Combine the flour, rice meal, baking powder, and remaining ¼ teaspoon salt in a medium bowl. Add the milk and 1 teaspoon oil, and stir until the dry ingredients are well moistened. The batter should be lumpy. Fold in the rice and parsley.

■ *4.* When the chicken is almost tender, drop the dumplings on top of the chicken by heaping tablespoonfuls. Cover tightly and simmer 10 minutes

Rice bran oil or olive oil

1 frying chicken, about 3 pounds, cut into eighths

1 large onion, coarsely chopped (about 1½ cups)

1 celery rib, coarsely chopped (about ⅔ cup)

¼ pound mushrooms, thinly sliced (about 1½ cups)

2 cups water

¾ teaspoon salt

¼ teaspoon dried thyme leaves

⅓ cup all-purpose flour

⅓ cup rice meal (see note)

½ teaspoon baking powder

without lifting the lid. Test a dumpling by cutting through to see if center is cooked. If necessary, cover and simmer 5 minutes longer. Serve immediately from the Dutch oven.

**Note:** To make rice meal, place brown or white regular or aromatic rice in the container of a blender and process until the consistency of cornmeal. Do not use a food processor. A measured amount of rice will make about the same amount of meal.

¼ cup milk

½ cup cooked white or brown rice (pages 14, 16)

2 tablespoons chopped fresh parsley

# shrimp pulao

*This curried shrimp and rice dish was inspired by a recipe that our friend Alice Hadler discovered while living abroad.*

*4 servings*

- *1.* For the seasoned rice, bring the water to a boil over high heat. Tie the cloves, peppercorns, cardamom, if desired, and cinnamon together in cheesecloth. Add to the boiling water along with the rice, cover, reduce the heat, and cook 15 to 20 minutes, until the liquid is absorbed and the rice is tender.
- *2.* While the rice is cooking, prepare the curried shrimp by heating the butter in a skillet. Add the tomatoes, garam masala, chili powder, ginger, and salt to taste. Cook 5 minutes, stirring frequently. About 5 minutes before the rice is done, add the shrimp to the skillet and cook over medium-high heat until the shrimp are pink. Taste and adjust seasonings.
- *3.* Serve the curried shrimp over the seasoned rice.

- *Seasoned Rice*

2 cups water

4 whole cloves

4 peppercorns

4 whole cardamom pods (optional)

Small stick cinnamon

1 cup white Basmati rice (see note)

- *Curried Shrimp*

4 tablespoons (½ stick) unsalted butter

2 large ripe tomatoes, peeled, seeded, and chopped

1 tablespoon garam masala

2 teaspoons chili powder

1 teaspoon ground ginger

Salt

1 pound medium shrimp, peeled and deveined

**Variation:** If you don't have garam masala, use 4 teaspoons hot curry powder instead of the garam masala, chili powder, and ground ginger, and serve over hot rice.

**Note:** If using imported Basmati, rinse it in several changes of water. This is unnecessary for U.S. Basmati.

Garam masala *is*

*a blend of ground*

*cardamom,*

*cloves, cinnamon,*

*cumin, nutmeg,*

*and black pepper.*

*In India, where*

*it is traditionally*

*used, the amount of*

*each spice varies*

*according to*

*personal preference.*

# skillet pork chops and rice

*This family one-dish-meal, a favorite in the forties, adapts well to the new leaner pork.*

*4 servings*

■ *1.* Heat the oil in a large skillet. Saute the pork chops until golden on both sides, about 6 to 8 minutes. Remove the chops to a plate.

■ *2.* Saute the onion in the same skillet until golden, about 5 minutes. Drain and discard as much fat as possible. Stir in the rice and 1 cup water. Bring to a boil.

■ *3.* Stir together the marjoram, salt, and pepper. Stir half of the seasoning mixture into the rice; place the chops on top of the rice and sprinkle with the remaining seasoning. Cover the skillet and cook over low heat for 20 minutes. Add tomatoes, continue cooking 25 minutes longer, adding more water if necessary.

■ *4.* Slice the ends from the pepper and finely chop them. Cut the center of the pepper into 4 rings; discard the seeds and membranes. Place a pepper

1 teaspoon rice bran oil or olive oil

4 well-trimmed center-cut pork chops, ½ inch thick (about 1¼ pounds)

1 large onion, sliced (about 1½ cups)

¾ cup brown rice

Water

½ teaspoon dried marjoram leaves

½ teaspoon salt

¼ teaspoon freshly ground black pepper

1 8-ounce can peeled tomatoes

1 large green bell pepper

½ cup ketchup or mild salsa (see note)

ring on top of each pork chop; sprinkle the chopped pepper around the edge of the skillet. Place a tablespoon of ketchup or salsa in the center of each pepper ring. Cover and cook 10 to 15 minutes longer, or until the chops and rice are tender and most of the liquid is absorbed.

**Note:** Use ketchup for the old-fashioned version, salsa for the new.

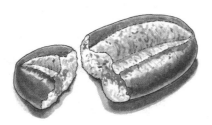

# shrimp etouffée

*4 servings*

- *1.* Heat the butter in a large skillet. Stir in the flour and cook, while stirring, until the mixture *(roux)* is reddish brown, about 5 minutes. Add the onion, celery, green pepper, and mushrooms. Cook until vegetables start to brown, about 5 minutes.
- *2.* Stir in the broth, chopped tomato, basil, thyme, salt to taste, black pepper, cayenne, Worcestershire sauce, and Tabasco. Bring to a boil while stirring and cook until thickened, about 1 minute. Fold in the shrimp; cook about 10 minutes over medium heat or until the shrimp are pink and firm.
- *3.* Taste and adjust seasonings; serve etouffée over hot, cooked rice.

**Note:** If you split the shrimp in half lengthwise, they will curl when cooked and appear to be twice as plentiful.

2 tablespoons unsalted butter

2 tablespoons all-purpose flour

1 medium onion, chopped (about 1 cup)

1 celery rib, sliced (about ⅔ cup)

1 medium green pepper, cored, seeded, and chopped (about ¾ cup)

¼ pound mushrooms, sliced (about 1½ cups)

1 cup chicken broth or water

1 medium tomato, chopped (about ¾ cup)

1 teaspoon dried basil

½ teaspoon dried thyme leaves

¼ to ½ teaspoon salt to taste

¼ teaspoon freshly ground black pepper

¼ teaspoon cayenne (ground red) pepper

1 teaspoon Worcestershire sauce

1 teaspoon Tabasco

1½ pounds medium shrimp, peeled and deveined

2 cups cooked brown or white rice (pages 16, 14), hot

# main
# dishes

*"Winter was coming and there would be no food, not even the poor remnants of the vegetables from the neighbors' gardens. They must have dried peas and sorghum and meal and rice and— and—oh, so many things."*

*Margaret Mitchell,*
Gone With the Wind,
*1936*

# sausage frittata

*6 servings*

■ *1.* Heat the sausage in an 8-inch skillet until cooked through. Remove from skillet and set aside. Discard all but about 2 tablespoons fat from the skillet. Add the pepper and onion, and saute over medium heat until the onion is very soft, about 10 minutes. Remove half the onion and pepper from the skillet and set aside. Return half the sausage to the skillet along with half the rice. Press to form an even layer. Spread the remaining sausage, onion, and pepper over the layer, then top with the remaining rice.

■ *2.* In a bowl, combine the eggs, milk, salt, and pepper. Pour over the rice, set the skillet over medium heat, and cook until the eggs are set around the edges, about 5 minutes. Sprinkle with cheese, cover, and let cook until the cheese is melted. Or place under a hot broiler until the cheese is melted. and the eggs are set.

■ *3.* Cut into wedges and serve.

½ pound spicy sausage, sliced into thin rounds

1 medium red bell pepper, cored, seeded, and sliced (about ¾ cup)

1 medium onion, sliced (about 1 cup)

2 cups cooked brown or white rice (pages 16, 14)

8 eggs

¼ cup milk

Salt and freshly ground black pepper to taste

½ cup grated sharp Cheddar cheese

**Variation:** Ratatouille Frittata. In place of the sausage, onion, and pepper, substitute your favorite ratatouille. Layer it with the rice and sprinkle with freshly grated Parmesan instead of Cheddar.

# kedgeree

*Kedgeree is an English breakfast that originated in India, usually made with kippers. This version uses the more readily available smoked whitefish.*

*6 servings*

- *1.* Preheat the oven to 350°F.
- *2.* Toss together the rice, fish, and parsley in a 1-quart ovenproof casserole. In a bowl, combine the butter, half-and-half, and curry powder to taste. Pour over the rice mixture. Sprinkle with the chopped eggs.
- *3.* Bake in the preheated oven for 30 minutes or until hot.

**3 cups cooked brown or white rice (pages 16, 14)**

**¾ pound smoked fish, flaked**

**¾ cup chopped fresh parsley**

**3 tablespoons unsalted butter, melted**

**6 tablespoons half-and-half**

**2 to 3 tablespoons curry powder**

**3 hard-cooked eggs, yolks and whites finely chopped**

# cabbage rolls

*Because the filling is precooked, these cabbage rolls can be cooked quickly and enjoyed while the cabbage is still sweet and slightly crisp.*

*8 rolls, 4 servings*

■ *1.* Thoroughly rinse the cabbage leaves. Using a meat mallet or the handle of a kitchen knife, flatten the large rib in each leaf. Bring water to a boil in a 2-quart saucepan. Add the cabbage, cover, and cook 5 to 7 minutes or until the leaves are flexible. Remove to a collander using tongs or a slotted spatula. Measure and reserve 1½ cups cooking liquid. Discard remaining liquid.

■ *2.* In the same saucepan, combine the reserved cooking liquid, the rice, basil, salt, and pepper. Bring to a boil over high heat; reduce heat to low, cover, and cook 15 minutes or until the rice is just tender and the liquid is absorbed.

■ *3.* Saute the bacon in a medium skillet until the pieces begin to curl. Add the scallions and red pepper; saute until the bacon is crisp and the

8 large cabbage leaves

2 cups water

½ cup long grain white rice

¼ teaspoon dried basil

¼ teaspoon salt

⅛ teaspoon freshly ground black pepper

¼ pound sliced bacon, coarsely chopped

2 scallions, finely chopped (about ¼ cup)

½ small red bell pepper, cored, seeded, and finely chopped (about ¼ cup)

1 14½-ounce can stewed tomatoes

vegetables are lightly browned. Drain off as much fat as possible; then stir in the uncooked rice.

■ 4. Place the drained cabbage leaves on a flat surface; evenly divide the rice mixture onto the leaves. Fold the sides of the cabbage leaves in, then roll up, starting from the thickest end, to make a roll about 3 inches long.

■ 5. In the same skillet, bring the stewed tomatoes to a boil. Place the cabbage rolls into the tomatoes. Cover and cook over low heat until the cabbage leaves are crisp-tender, about 15 to 20 minutes. Serve with some tomatoes spooned over the rolls.

# rizza romano

*This rice pizza is a meal in itself.*

*6 servings*

- *1.* Preheat the oven to 400°F. Generously grease an 11-inch pizza pan or a large cookie sheet.
- *2.* Heat the oil in a medium skillet. Add the onion and garlic and saute until golden. Stir in the tomatoes, pepper, ½ teaspoon basil, ¼ teaspoon oregano, and salt. Cook, stirring occasionally, until the moisture has evaporated, about 10 minutes.
- *3.* In a medium bowl, stir together the rice, egg, and remaining basil and oregano. Turn onto the prepared pan; cover with wax paper or plastic wrap, and press rice firmly and evenly into an 11-inch round with a rim. Remove the wax paper or plastic wrap. Sprinkle half of the mozzarella over the rice. Top with the tomato mixture, the remaining mozzarella cheese, and the Romano cheese.
- *4.* Bake for 20 to 25 minutes or until the cheese is browned and bubbly. Remove from the oven and serve immediately.

1 tablespoon rice bran oil or olive oil

1 small onion, chopped (about ½ cup)

3 garlic cloves, sliced

2 medium, ripe tomatoes, chopped (about 1½ cups)

1 medium green bell pepper, cored, seeded, and chopped (about ¾ cup)

1 teaspoon dried basil

½ teaspoon dried oregano leaves

¼ teaspoon salt

3 cups cooked brown or white rice (pages 16, 14)

1 egg

8 ounces mozzarella cheese, shredded

2 tablespoons freshly grated Romano cheese

# stuffed peppers

*6 servings*

■ *1.* Cut each red pepper in half lengthwise; discard the seeds and membranes. In a large skillet, bring 1 inch of water to a boil over medium heat. Add the red peppers, cut side down; cover and cook for 10 minutes or until crisp-tender. Drain well and arrange in a shallow baking dish or ovenproof platter.

■ *2.* Heat the same skillet until dry. Add the oil, then the ground beef, scallions, and green pepper. Saute, stirring, until the beef is browned. Drain off any fat. Stir in the rice, basil, salt, pepper, and peas.

■ *3.* Preheat the oven to 400°F.

■ *4.* Stir together the tomatoes and cornstarch in a small saucepan until the cornstarch is dissolved. Heat, while stirring, until the mixture boils and is thickened. Fold into the rice mixture and divide among the pepper halves. Top with cheese, if desired, and bake for 20 minutes. Serve immediately.

3 large red bell peppers (about 1½ pounds)

1 teaspoon vegetable oil or rice bran oil

½ pound ground beef

4 scallions, chopped (about ½ cup)

1 small green bell pepper

2 cups cooked brown or white rice (pages 16, 14)

½ teaspoon dried basil

½ teaspoon salt

⅛ teaspoon freshly ground black pepper

½ cup frozen peas

1 14½-ounce can stewed tomatoes

1 tablespoon cornstarch

½ cup grated Jarlsberg cheese (optional)

# rice sausage

*These preservative-free, spicy sausages are good any time.*

*12 6-inch links or 2½-inch patties*

- *1.* Combine the turkey, rice, scallions, parsley, salt, Tabasco, pepper, thyme, and optional sage in a large bowl.
- *2.* Shape into twelve 6-inch sausage-shaped rolls or 2½-inch patties. If stuffing into casings, cut the casing into 3 pieces; wash natural casings thoroughly. If using collagen casings, follow manufacturer's directions. Using a sausage stuffer, stuff sausage mixture into the casings. Twist or tie into 6-inch links.
- *3.* To cook sausages, heat oil in a large skillet. If sausages are in casings, pierce several times with the tines of a fork. Saute the sausages, several at a time, until golden brown on all sides and cooked through, about 10 to 12 minutes in all. Cooked sausages can be frozen for up to 2 months and reheated in a skillet or microwave before serving.

¾ pound ground turkey

1½ cups cooked brown or white rice (pages 16, 14)

2 scallions, finely chopped (about ¼ cup)

¼ cup chopped fresh parsley

1 teaspoon salt

¼ to ½ teaspoon Tabasco

½ teaspoon cracked black pepper

¼ teaspoon dried thyme leaves

¼ teaspoon rubbed sage (optional)

3 yards natural sheep casings or small collagen casings (optional; see mail order sources, page 127)

2 teaspoons rice bran oil or olive oil, for frying

# porcupine meatballs

*It was discovered that if you put raw rice in your meatballs and cook them in a pressure cooker, the force of the steam would make the rice pop out from the surface of the meatballs, resembling the quills on a porcupine.*

*6 servings*

■ *1.* Combine the turkey, rice, onion, garlic, dill, salt, and pepper in a bowl. Form into 24 balls.

■ *2.* Bring the tomatoes to a boil in a 4-quart pressure cooker. Add the meatballs. Cover and heat to 15 pounds pressure, being careful to follow manufacturer's safety directions.

■ *3.* Cook meatballs 10 minutes; remove from the heat and set aside until pressure has gone down naturally.

■ *4.* Remove the lid of the pressure cooker. With a slotted spoon, place the meatballs in a serving bowl. Stir the water into the flour and stir the mixture into the tomatoes in the pressure cooker. Heat to boiling, stirring until thickened. Pour over the meatballs and serve.

1 pound ground turkey

½ cup long grain white rice or any rice blend that cooks in 15 to 20 minutes

1 small onion, finely chopped (about ½ cup)

2 garlic cloves, finely chopped

½ teaspoon dried dill

½ teaspoon salt

¼ teaspoon cracked black pepper

1 15-ounce can whole tomatoes

¼ cup water

1 tablespoon all-purpose flour

# risotto

*"Risotto is a uniquely Italian technique for cooking rice. There are so many things you can do with risotto that it is almost a cuisine all by itself."*

Marcella Hazan,
The Classic Italian
Cookbook, *1979*

# basic risotto

*6 servings*

■ *1.* Saute the onion in the butter and oil in a 2-quart saucepan over medium heat until soft, about 5 minutes. Add the rice and cook over medium heat until the rice is opaque and pearl-like.

■ *2.* Add the hot broth, ½ cup at a time, stirring constantly with a wooden spoon and waiting until the broth is absorbed before adding more. Continue adding broth ½ cup at a time until the rice is cooked but still al dente, or firm to the bite. (All the broth may not be needed.) This will take 20 to 25 minutes.

■ *3.* Remove from the heat, stir in the ½ cup Parmesan, and serve immediately. If desired, pass additional Parmesan at the table.

½ small onion, finely minced (about ¼ cup)

2 tablespoons unsalted butter

2 tablespoons olive oil

2 cups rice, preferably Arborio

6 to 8 cups chicken broth, simmering

½ cup freshly grated Parmesan cheese, plus additional for the table

# risotto with asparagus

*6 servings*

- *1.* Trim and rinse the asparagus. Peel the tough part of the stems or discard. Cut off the tips and set aside. Cut the stems into ½-inch pieces and set aside.
- *2.* Saute the shallots in 1½ tablespoons of the butter and the oil in a 2-quart saucepan over medium high heat until softened, about 5 minutes. Stir in the asparagus stems, salt, pepper, and rice. Cook over medium heat until the rice is opaque and pearl-like, about 3 minutes.
- *3.* Add the wine and cook, while stirring, until it is completely absorbed. Then add the hot broth, ½ cup at a time, stirring constantly with a wooden spoon and waiting until the broth is absorbed before adding more. After the rice has been cooking for 20 minutes, add the asparagus tips. Continue adding broth ½ cup at a time and stirring gently, until the rice is cooked but still al dente, or firm to the bite. (All the broth may not be needed.)

¾ pound fresh asparagus

¼ cup finely minced shallots

3 tablespoons unsalted butter

2 tablespoons olive oil

Salt and freshly ground black pepper to taste

2 cups rice, preferably Arborio

½ cup dry white wine

Approximately 6½ cups chicken broth, simmering

½ cup freshly grated Parmesan cheese, plus additional for the table

■ *4.* Remove from the heat, stir in the ½ cup Parmesan, and serve immediately. If desired, pass additional Parmesan at the table.

## Creamy Risotto

■

*Risotto takes about 20 to 25 minutes to prepare. When cooking a risotto, the rice is first browned in oil and butter, often with some onions or shallots. Instead of adding liquid all at once as in a pilaf, simmering broth is added very slowly, about ½ cup at a time, and the mixture is stirred continuously until the rice is very tender but still firm. The resulting rice dish is very creamy— sort of a savory rice pudding.*

*Arborio, a medium grain, highly glutinous rice, is preferred when making risotto. If Arborio is unavailable, parboiled long grain rice can be used. The resulting risotto, although not as creamy, is quite good.*

*The texture is better if made on the stove-top, but if it is made in the microwave (page 87), it doesn't require constant stirring.*

# risotto with sausage, artichokes, and peas

*4 servings*

- *1.* Saute the onion in the butter and oil in a 2-quart saucepan over medium heat until softened, about 5 minutes. Add the sausage meat and cook until it loses its pink color. Add the rice and cook over medium heat until it is opaque and pearl-like, about 3 minutes.
- *2.* Add the hot broth, ½ cup at a time, stirring constantly with a wooden spoon and waiting until the broth is absorbed before adding more. Continue adding broth ½ cup at a time until the rice is cooked but still al dente, or firm to the bite. (All the broth may not be needed.)
- *3.* Add the peas, artichokes, and ⅓ cup Parmesan. Stir until the vegetables are warmed through, then serve immediately. If desired, pass additional Parmesan at the table.

½ small onion, finely minced (about ¼ cup)

2 tablespoons unsalted butter

1 tablespoon olive oil

¼ pound sweet Italian sausage, casings removed

1½ cups rice, preferably Arborio

4 to 6 cups chicken broth, simmering

½ cup frozen peas, thawed

3 artichoke hearts, canned in water, sliced

⅓ cup freshly grated Parmesan cheese, plus additional for the table

# champagne
# risotto

*Serve this dish with champagne.*

*6 servings*

■ *1.* Saute the shallots in the butter in a 2-quart saucepan over medium heat until softened, about 5 minutes. Add the rice and cook over medium heat until the rice is opaque and pearl-like, about 3 minutes.

■ *2.* Add 1 cup of champagne and stir until it is completely absorbed. Then add the hot broth, ½ cup at a time, stirring constantly with a wooden spoon and waiting until the broth is absorbed before adding more. Continue adding broth ½ cup at a time until the rice is cooked but still al dente, or firm to the bite. (All the broth may not be needed.)

■ *3.* Add the remaining ¼ cup champagne and continue stirring until almost absorbed, about 2 minutes. Remove from the heat, stir in the half-and-half and the ½ cup Parmesan, and serve immediately. If desired, pass additional Parmesan at the table.

¼ cup finely minced shallots

4 tablespoons (½ stick) unsalted butter

1½ cups rice, preferably Arborio

1¼ cup brut (dry) champagne

3 to 5 cups chicken broth, simmering

¼ cup half-and-half

½ cup freshly grated Parmesan cheese, plus additional for the table

# green risotto

*This is our favorite risotto.*

*6 servings*

- *1.* Saute the scallions in 1 tablespoon of the butter and the oil in a 2-quart saucepan over medium heat until softened, about 5 minutes. Add the rice and garlic; cook over medium heat until the rice is opaque and pearl-like, about 3 minutes.
- *2.* Add the hot broth, ½ cup at a time, stirring constantly with a wooden spoon and waiting until the broth is absorbed before adding more.
- *3.* While the risotto is cooking, blend together the basil, spinach, parsley, and remaining 2 tablespoons butter in a food processor.
- *4.* Continue adding broth ½ cup at a time to the risotto until the rice is cooked but still al dente, or firm to the bite. (All the broth may not be needed.) Stir in the herb butter, ¼ cup Parmesan, the salt, and pepper. Serve immediately. If desired, pass additional Parmesan at the table.

⅓ cup finely minced scallions

3 tablespoons unsalted butter, softened

2 tablespoons olive oil

1 cup rice, preferably Arborio

2 garlic cloves, minced

3 to 4 cups chicken broth, simmering

½ cup loosely packed fresh basil leaves

1½ cups loosely packed spinach leaves

½ cup loosely packed parsley leaves, preferably Italian

¼ cup freshly grated Parmesan cheese, plus additional for the table

Salt and freshly ground black pepper to taste

# microwave risotto

*4 servings*

■ *1.* In a microwave-safe 8-inch square dish, heat the butter and oil at full power (100 percent) in a 500-watt or more microwave oven for 1 minute. Stir in the shallots and cook at full power for 2 minutes. Stir in the rice and cook at full power for 2 minutes.

■ *2.* Add the broth and cook, uncovered, at full power for 6 minutes. Stir well and continue to cook at full power for 7 minutes more. Remove from oven, let stand about 5 minutes, stirring frequently until the rice absorbs the liquid. Stir in the cheese. Serve immediately. If desired, pass additional Parmesan at the table.

Note: If your oven power is less than 500 watts, adjust the cooking times to 9 minutes after adding the broth and 10 minutes after stirring.

1½ tablespoons unsalted butter

1½ tablespoons olive oil

⅓ cup finely minced shallots

1 cup rice, preferably Arborio

3 cups chicken broth, simmering

¼ cup freshly grated Parmesan cheese, plus additional for the table

# pepper chèvre risotto with sun-dried tomatoes

*6 servings*

- *1.* Pour the boiling water over the sun-dried tomatoes and let stand 10 to 20 minutes, until soft. Drain and cut into thin strips.
- *2.* Saute the onion in the butter in a 2-quart saucepan over medium heat until softened, about 5 minutes. Add the rice and cook over medium heat until the rice is opaque and pearl-like, about 3 minutes.
- *3.* Add the hot broth, ½ cup at a time, stirring constantly with a wooden spoon and waiting until the broth is absorbed before adding more. Continue adding broth ½ cup at a time until the rice is cooked but still al dente, or firm to the bite. (All the broth may not be needed.)
- *4.* Remove from the heat, then stir in the sun-dried tomatoes, chèvre, and pepper until the chèvre is melted. Serve immediately, sprinkled with parsley, if desired.

½ cup boiling water

12 sun-dried tomatoes

½ small onion, finely minced (about ¼ cup)

2 tablespoons unsalted butter

2 cups rice, preferably Arborio

6 to 8 cups chicken broth, simmering

4 ounces chèvre at room temperature, cut in small pieces

1 teaspoon cracked black pepper

Chopped fresh parsley (optional)

# side dishes

"... on those rare evenings when I find myself in a place where the only alternative to sitting like a condemned man in the motel dining room is starvation, rolling into baked duck and dirty rice is something I've thought about a lot myself."

Calvin Trillin,
Third Helpings,
1983

# rice pilaf

*Use this master recipe to make an infinite number of dishes by changing the vegetables, spices, liquid, or by adding a favorite food. Elaborate pilaf-style dishes include Paella (pages 56, 58), Jambalaya (page 48), Green Rice (page 94), Nutty Rice Pilaf (page 95), and Shrimp Creole (page 50).*

*4–6 servings*

■ *1.* Heat the oil in a 2-quart saucepan. Add the onion and saute until translucent, about 5 minutes. Add the rice and cook, stirring constantly, until the rice is opaque and coated with the oil.

■ *2.* Add the broth and bring to a boil over high heat; stir, cover, reduce the heat, and cook 15 to 20 minutes, until the rice is tender and the liquid is absorbed.

1 tablespoon vegetable oil or rice bran oil

1 small onion, chopped (about ½ cup)

1 cup long grain white rice

2 cups broth or water

Salt and freshly ground black pepper to taste

**Variations:** Saute celery, shallots, scallions, garlic, fennel, or green, red, or yellow pepper in addition to or in place of the onion. Toss in diced fresh tomatoes or blanched broccoli, peas, or cauliflower 5 minutes before the end of the cooking time. Add cooked chicken, shrimp, beef slices, feta cheese, Parmesan, or crabmeat 5 minutes before the end of the cooking time. Or vary the flavor by changing the liquid to half orange, half tomato, or half pineapple juice and half water. The list is endless.

*"... cooked rice was banished from Turkish kitchens for over a century. (Though, it must be told, contraband rice was often eaten on the sly. And the very word* pilau—*originally an acronym for the Greek work for 'plate' and the Latin for 'to praise'—implied that free-thinkers ate as they pleased.)"*

*Bert Greene,*

The Grains Cookbook,

*1988*

# rice and rivvels

*Rivvels are little pieces of egg noodle dough. Traditionally they are shaped like rice or the pasta* orzo *and used in soups. This rice and rivvels combination is a great side dish as is, or add meat and vegetables for a one-dish meal.*

*4 servings*

■ *1.* Combine the flour and salt in a small bowl. Add the egg and stir with a fork. Knead the mixture in the bowl until a smooth ball forms.

■ *2.* On a lightly floured surface, with a floured rolling pin, roll out the dough to form a 10-inch square. With a sharp knife, cut the dough into ¼-inch-wide strips. Cut across strips at ¼-inch intervals to divide the dough into ¼-inch squares. Toss squares lightly with a little flour to separate. If desired, roll each square between your palms to make a rice-shaped oval. Drop the squares or ovals into a strainer and shake off the excess flour.

½ cup all-purpose flour

⅛ teaspoon salt

1 egg, beaten

3½ cups chicken or beef broth, or salted water

½ cup long grain white rice

■ *3.* In a 2-quart saucepan, bring the broth to a boil; stir in the rice. Return to a boil, reduce heat to low, cover, and cook for 10 minutes. Stir in the rivvels; cook for 5 to 7 minutes or until the rice is tender and most of the broth is absorbed. Fluff with a fork and serve.

*Pennsylvania Dutch cooks make rivvels by hand rolling scraps of noodle dough or little pieces of a soft, crumbly dough, which has been made especially for the purpose. Because this process is so labor intensive, we found it easier to roll out the dough and cut it into pieces and either cook the little squares or hand roll them before cooking, depending upon available time.*

# green rice

*4–6 servings*

■ *1.* Heat the oil in a heavy 2-quart saucepan. Add the scallions and green pepper and saute until softened, about 2 minutes. Add the rice, stir to coat with the oil, then add the water or broth, salt, and pepper. Bring to a boil over high heat; stir, reduce the heat, cover, and cook 20 minutes or until all liquid is absorbed and the rice is tender.

■ *2.* In a medium bowl, mix the parsley, yogurt, lime juice and zest, and cayenne. Add the warm rice, toss well, and taste and adjust seasonings.

**Variation:** Substitute 1 4-ounce can diced green chilies for the green pepper, 2 tablespoons chopped fresh cilantro plus ¼ cup chopped fresh parsley for the parsley, and add ½ teaspoon ground cumin when adding the cayenne pepper.

To fire up the flavor of the cooked rice, add a few drops of Tabasco or other hot pepper sauce to the cooking liquid.

1 tablespoon olive oil

1 cup chopped scallions, including green tops

½ medium green bell pepper, cored, seeded, and chopped (generous ⅓ cup)

1 cup U.S. aromatic rice

2 cups water or chicken broth

½ teaspoon salt (omit if using canned broth)

Freshly ground black pepper to taste

½ cup chopped fresh parsley

2 tablespoons plain yogurt

1 tablespoon freshly squeezed lime juice

1 teaspoon grated lime zest

Cayenne (ground red) pepper to taste

# nutty rice pilaf

*To make ahead, just double the rec-
ipe, press into a well-greased 8-cup
mold, and refrigerate until needed.
Bring to room temperature, then
bake, in the mold, in a 400°F. oven for
15 minutes. Set aside for 5 minutes,
then unmold onto a serving platter.*

*4–6 servings*

■ *1.* Heat the oils in a heavy 2-quart
saucepan. Add the pine nuts and
saute until golden. Remove with a
slotted spoon and set aside. Add the
onion, red pepper, and garlic to the
pan and saute until the onion is translucent, about 3 minutes.

■ *2.* Add the rice, stir to coat with
oil, then add the broth, salt, pepper,
and saffron. Bring to a boil over high
heat, cover, reduce the heat, and cook
for 35 minutes.

■ *3.* Mix in the currants and the reserved pine nuts, cover, and let cook
an additional 5 minutes, or until the
rice is tender and the liquid is absorbed. Serve.

1 tablespoon Oriental sesame oil

1 tablespoon vegetable oil

¼ cup pine nuts (pignoli)

1 medium onion, coarsely chopped
(about 1 cup)

1 medium red bell pepper, cored,
seeded, and cut into 3-inch julienne
strips (¾ cup)

1 garlic clove, minced

1 cup rice blend (should include
wild and brown rice)

2 cups chicken broth or water

½ teaspoon salt (omit salt if using
canned broth)

Freshly ground black pepper to taste

½ teaspoon saffron threads

¼ cup currants or raisins

# dirty rice

*The added chicken gizzard and livers darken this spicy Cajun dish, hence its name "dirty."*

*4–6 servings*

■ *1.* Heat the oil in a heavy 2-quart saucepan. Add the gizzards and cook over high heat until thoroughly browned, about 5 minutes. Add the livers and cook until they lose their pink color, 1 to 2 minutes. Add the onion, green pepper, celery, garlic, cayenne, salt, pepper, paprika, cumin, and mustard. Reduce the heat to medium and cook, stirring constantly, for about 5 minutes.

■ *2.* Add the broth, bring to a boil, and stir to loosen any particles stuck to the bottom of the pan. Add the rice, cover, reduce heat to low, and cook for 20 minutes or until the liquid is absorbed and the rice is tender. Taste and adjust seasonings. Sprinkle with parsley and serve.

2 tablespoons vegetable oil

½ pound chicken gizzards, ground

½ pound chicken livers, ground

1 medium onion, finely chopped (about 1 cup)

1 medium green pepper, cored, seeded, and finely chopped (about ¾ cup)

1 celery rib, finely chopped (about ⅔ cup)

2 garlic cloves, minced

1½ teaspoons cayenne (ground red) pepper

1 teaspoon salt (omit half if using canned broth)

1 teaspoon freshly ground black pepper

1 teaspoon sweet paprika

½ teaspoon ground cumin

½ teaspoon dry mustard

2 cups chicken broth

1 cup U.S. aromatic rice

½ cup minced fresh parsley

# pesto rice

*If you like pesto on pasta, you're sure to love it on rice. If you have any leftover Pesto Rice, toss it with some plain yogurt for a refreshing cold rice salad.*

*6 servings*

■ *1.* In a food processor or blender, mince the garlic, basil, Parmesan, parsley, and pine nuts for the pesto. Add the oil while the machine is running and process until blended.

■ *2.* If not using immediately, store in a covered container in the refrigerator for up to a week, or freeze for 3 months. Makes about 1 cup pesto.

■ *3.* Bring the broth to a boil over high heat; add the rice and salt, if using. Reduce the heat, cover, and cook for 15 to 20 minutes or until all liquid is absorbed and rice is tender.

■ *4.* Toss the warm rice with the pesto. Sprinkle with Parmesan cheese to taste and, if desired, toss with the cucumber and tomato.

▪ **Pesto**

**1 garlic clove, peeled**

**½ cup packed, fresh basil leaves**

**¼ cup freshly grated Parmesan cheese**

**2 tablespoons chopped fresh parsley**

**1 tablespoon pine nuts (pignoli)**

**½ cup olive oil**

▪ **Rice**

**2 cups chicken broth or water**

**1 cup long grain white rice**

**½ teaspoon salt (omit if using canned broth)**

**Freshly grated Parmesan cheese**

**1 medium cucumber, peeled, seeded, and diced (optional)**

**1 large tomato, peeled, seeded, and diced (optional)**

# coconut rice

*Traditionally, coconut rice is served as part of an Indonesian rice table or* rijsttafel, *often consisting of thirty or more dishes. It is also great as a side dish served with chicken or fish.*

*6–8 servings*

- *1.* Bring coconut milk to a boil in a 2-quart saucepan over high heat. Add rice, salt, bay leaf, turmeric, coriander, and pepper to taste. Stir, cover, reduce heat, and cook about 20 minutes, until the rice is tender and liquid is absorbed.
- *2.* Taste and adjust seasonings.

Note: Coconut milk can be found in Oriental or Indian grocery stores. Or it can be made by soaking ½ cup shredded fresh coconut in ½ cup boiling water for 20 minutes, then blending it in a blender or food processor until smooth. Strain.

3 cups coconut milk (see note)

1½ cups Jasmine or other aromatic rice

½ teaspoon salt

1 bay leaf

½ teaspoon ground turmeric

½ teaspoon ground coriander

Freshly ground black pepper

# chinese fried rice

*This is a Chinese classic.*

*4–6 servings*

■ *1.* With your fingers, separate and loosen the rice so the grains don't stick together.

■ *2.* Heat the oil in deep skillet or wok over high heat. Add the sausages or ham and stir-fry (or toss) until warmed, about 2 minutes. Add the rice and stir-fry without browning until warmed, about 2 minutes.

■ *3.* Make a well in the center of the rice, add the eggs, and stir constantly until soft scrambled. Add the peas, water chestnuts, oyster sauce, soy sauce, and sesame oil. Toss to blend. Taste and adjust the seasonings. Add the scallions and serve.

**Variations:** Use any leftover meat, poultry, or seafood, such as shrimp, crab, or lobster, in place of the sausages. Use bamboo shoots, bean sprouts, mushrooms, pimientos, onions, peppers, or blanched string beans or celery in place of some or all of peas and water chestnuts.

**4 cups cooked rice, cold**

**¼ cup vegetable oil**

**¾ cup diced Chinese sausages or cooked ham**

**2 eggs, lightly beaten**

**¾ cup frozen peas, thawed**

**½ cup diced water chestnuts**

**2 tablespoons oyster sauce**

**1 teaspoon soy sauce**

**1 teaspoon Oriental sesame oil**

**2 scallions, minced**

# hoppin' john

*While there are many tales about the origin of the name Hoppin' John, none of them has been proven. What is true is that this flavorful combination of black-eyed peas and rice has been a Southern favorite for many years. Traditionally served on New Year's Day for good luck, it is so mouth-watering you will want to make it more often.*

*6 servings*

■ *1.* Melt the butter or saute the salt pork in a large heavy skillet. Add the onion and garlic and saute, stirring constantly, until the onion is golden, about 5 minutes. If using the salt pork, drain off the excess fat.

■ *2.* Rinse the black-eyed peas; discard any small stones. Add black-eyed peas, rice, and salt to the skillet. (If using salt pork, use the least amount of salt.) Gradually stir in the water.

■ *3.* Bring to a boil over high heat. Reduce heat, cover, and cook 50 to 60 minutes, or until the black-eyed peas and rice are tender and all the liquid

1 tablespoon unsalted butter *or* ¼ pound salt pork, coarsely chopped

1 medium onion, chopped (about 1 cup)

2 garlic cloves, finely chopped

¾ cup dried black-eyed peas

¾ cup brown rice

½ to 1½ teaspoons salt

4 cups water

is absorbed. Fluff with a fork and serve.

Note: Black-eyed peas cook more quickly than other dried legumes and do not need to be presoaked.

# rice grits and cheese

*6 servings*

■ *1.* Preheat the oven to 400°F. Grease a 1½-quart baking dish.

■ *2.* Combine the milk and egg in a medium bowl. Stir in the grits and chilies.

■ *3.* Layer one third of the grits and one third of the cheese in the baking dish; repeat twice. Bake 25 to 30 minutes or until bubbly and well browned. Serve immediately.

1 cup milk

1 egg, lightly beaten

3 cups cooked, salted rice grits or rice couscous

1 4-ounce can chopped mild green chilies, drained

1½ cups grated Cheddar cheese

# wild rice and corn custard

*6 servings*

■ *1.* Preheat the oven to 350°F. Lightly butter a 1½-quart casserole.

■ *2.* Saute the onion and pepper in butter in a small skillet until the onion is golden, about 5 minutes. In a small bowl, beat the eggs until frothy. Blend in the milk, sauteed pepper and onion, salt, sugar, wild rice, and corn. Turn into a buttered casserole.

■ *3.* Bake the casserole for 35 to 40 minutes or until the center seems firm when the dish is jiggled. Serve immediately.

1 tablespoon unsalted butter

1 small onion, finely chopped (about ½ cup)

½ medium green bell pepper, cored, seeded, and finely chopped (generous ⅓ cup)

2 eggs

2 cups milk

½ teaspoon salt

1 teaspoon sugar

1 cup cooked wild rice (page 18)

1 cup frozen whole kernel corn

# rice stuffing

*Use this flavorful rice mixture in place of the usual bread to stuff the cavity of a 6-pound roasting chicken or a 6- to 8-pound turkey.*

*Makes 4 cups*

■ *1.* Heat the butter in a large skillet. Add the onion, pepper, and garlic and saute until golden, about 5 minutes. Gradually stir in the water, rice, salt, and thyme. Bring to a boil over high heat; reduce the heat to low, cover, and cook 15 to 20 minutes or until the rice is just tender and the liquid is absorbed.

■ *2.* Fluff the rice with a fork; stir in the walnuts and sesame seeds. Place the stuffing into the bird just before roasting.

**Note:** To toast sesame seeds, spread them out in an 8-inch baking pan and place in a 350°F. oven for 5 to 7 minutes, until golden, stirring once.

1 tablespoon unsalted butter

1 small onion, finely chopped (about ½ cup)

½ medium green bell pepper, cored, seeded, and finely chopped (generous ⅓ cup)

1 garlic clove, finely chopped

2 cups water

1 cup long grain white rice

½ teaspoon salt

½ teaspoon dried thyme leaves

½ cup coarsely chopped walnuts

2 tablespoons toasted sesame seeds (see note)

# polo

*A Middle Eastern rice dish, "known as rice with a golden crust."*

*4–6 servings*

■ *1.* Fill a 3-quart saucepan with 2 quarts cold water and bring to a boil. Add the rice and 1¼ teaspoon salt, stir, and boil uncovered over high heat, stirring occasionally for 8 minutes, or until the rice is firm but no longer brittle. Drain, rinse in cold water to stop the cooking, and toss with the dill and remaining ¼ teaspoon salt.

■ *2.* In the same saucepan, bring 3 tablespoons water and 5 tablespoons butter to a boil. Pour into a cup and set aside. Saute the onion in the remaining tablespoon butter in the saucepan until wilted, about 2 minutes. Add half the reserved water-butter, then stir in the rice, mounding it up in a cone shape. Using the handle of a wooden spoon, make a deep hole in the center of the cone.

1 cup long grain rice

1½ teaspoons salt

½ cup finely chopped fresh dill

3 tablespoons water

6 tablespoons (¾ stick) unsalted butter

1 medium onion, finely diced (about 1 cup)

■ *3.* Cook, covered, over medium heat for 5 minutes. Uncover, pour the remaining water-butter evenly over the rice, cover, and let cook over very low heat for 40 minutes, until the rice is tender and a golden crust forms on the bottom. Remove from heat and let stand, covered, for 5 minutes to loosen the crust. Fluff and serve the steamed rice along with some of the crust.

## The Golden Crust

■

*Middle Easterners have an unusual method for cooking rice that produces a thin golden crust—*tah digue—*on the bottom of the pan. The rice is boiled for a short time, drained, and then mounded into a cone shape in a saucepan. It is steamed for about three quarters of an hour, allowing the* tah digue *to form. A Middle Eastern cook's reputation is either made or broken by the quality of the* tah digue, *which should be golden in color—never burnt or dark brown.*

*Plain steamed rice with a crust is called* chelo. *When accompaniments are cooked with the steamed rice, they're known as* polo. *Some common* polo *additions include onions, yogurt, dried fruits, sour cherries, almonds, baby lima beans, lentils, fava beans, saffron, and poultry or various meats, with the exception of pork.*

# puddings and desserts

*"A Rice Pudding. One quarter of a pound rice, a stick of cinnamon, to a quart of milk (stirred often to keep from burning) and boil quick, cook and add·half a nutmeg, 4 spoons rose-water, 8 eggs; butter or puff paste a dish and pour the above composition into it, and bake one and one-half hour."*

*Amelia Simmons,*
*American Cooking, 1796*

# quick rice pudding

*4 servings*

- *1.* Bring the water, raisins, honey, cinnamon, and salt to a boil in a 1-quart saucepan. Stir in the rice and almonds. Spoon into a 1-quart serving dish. Set aside 10 minutes to cool.
- *2.* Fold in the yogurt. Serve warm or refrigerate and serve chilled.

¼ cup water

¼ cup raisins

2 tablespoons honey

½ teaspoon ground cinnamon

⅛ teaspoon salt

2 cups cooked brown or white rice (pages 16, 14)

¼ cup coarsely chopped unblanched almonds

8 ounces vanilla lowfat yogurt

# slow rice pudding

- *1.* Preheat the oven to 300°F. Lightly butter a shallow 1½-quart baking dish.
- *2.* In a 1-quart saucepan, scald the milk. In the baking dish, stir together the milk, rice, brown sugar, cinnamon, and salt.
- *3.* Bake the rice mixture for 2 to 2¼ hours, stirring once after the first half hour.
- *4.* When the rice is tender and all the milk is absorbed, remove to a wire rack to cool to room temperature. Serve at room temperature or refrigerate to serve chilled.

1 quart milk

¾ cup short or medium grain white rice

¼ cup firmly packed light brown sugar

½ teaspoon ground cinnamon

¼ teaspoon salt

# chocolate rice pudding

*Make it sweet or bittersweet, this special rice pudding is a chocolate-lover's delight.*

*6 servings*

■ *1.* Bring the water to a boil in a heavy 2-quart saucepan. Stir in the rice, salt, and cinnamon. Cover and cook over low heat until all the water is absorbed, about 12 to 15 minutes.

■ *2.* Stir the milk, sugar, and chocolate into the cooked rice. Heat to boiling over medium heat, stirring constantly. Stir the heavy cream into the cornstarch and add to the rice mixture. Cook, continuing to stir, until the pudding thickens. Cook 1 minute longer. Remove from the heat and stir in the vanilla.

■ *3.* Turn the pudding into a heatproof 1-quart serving bowl. Cool 15 minutes, then serve warm; or cool completely and refrigerate to serve chilled.

½ cup water

½ cup short or medium grain white rice

½ teaspoon salt

½ teaspoon ground cinnamon

1 cup milk

¼ to ⅓ cup sugar to taste

2 ounces semisweet or unsweetened chocolate

½ cup heavy cream

1 teaspoon cornstarch

2 teaspoons vanilla extract

# butterscotch
# rice pudding

*4 servings*

■ *1.* Bring the water to a boil in a heavy 2-quart saucepan. Add the rice and salt. Cook, covered, over low heat until all the water is absorbed, about 15 minutes.

■ *2.* Add the milk and cook over low heat for 10 minutes, until the milk has come to a boil. Remove from the heat and stir in the vanilla.

■ *3.* Preheat the oven to 350°F. Lightly butter a 1-quart shallow baking dish.

■ *4.* In a small skillet, melt the butter, then stir in the heavy cream and the brown sugar. Bring to a boil, then cook 2 minutes, stirring constantly. Fold into the rice mixture. Turn into the prepared dish.

■ *5.* Bake for 20 to 25 minutes, or until the pudding has a golden crust and is thickened. Cool on a wire rack for 15 minutes and serve warm, or cool completely and refrigerate to serve chilled.

1 cup water

⅓ cup short or medium grain white rice

¼ teaspoon salt

1½ cups milk

1 teaspoon vanilla extract

2 tablespoons unsalted butter

½ cup heavy cream

⅓ cup firmly packed dark brown sugar

# the best rice pudding

*This can be habit-forming.*

*6 servings*

■ *1.* Bring the water to a boil in a 2-quart saucepan. Add the rice, vanilla bean, and salt. Cook 10 minutes.

■ *2.* Add the milk and cook over very low heat until the rice is tender, about 10 minutes.

■ *3.* Preheat the oven to 350°F. Lightly butter a 1½-quart shallow baking dish.

■ *4.* In a small bowl, combine the cream, sugar, eggs, and cherries, then fold into the rice mixture. Remove the vanilla bean and pour the rice mixture into the buttered baking dish. Sprinkle with cinnamon.

■ *5.* Place the baking dish into a larger baking pan in the oven. Pour boiling water into the larger baking pan to a depth of 1 inch. Bake 30 to 45 minutes, or until the pudding is firm and the top surface is golden brown. Cool to room temperature on a wire rack. Serve at room temperature or refrigerate, covered, to serve chilled.

1 cup water

½ cup short or medium grain white rice

½ vanilla bean, split

¼ teaspoon salt

2 cups milk

1 cup heavy cream

½ cup sugar

2 eggs

½ cup raisins or dried sour cherries

¼ teaspoon ground cinnamon

111

# riz à l'imperatrice

*This gelled rice pudding, a classic French dessert, was especially popular in the early 1900s. It still makes a spectacular presentation. We have substituted dried fruit for the more traditional candied peels and citron; however you can use any dried or candied fruit you like.*

*8 servings*

■ *1.* Bring the water to a boil in a 2-quart saucepan. Add the rice, vanilla bean, and salt. Cook, covered, for 10 minutes over low heat.

■ *2.* Add the milk and dried cherries and cook, uncovered, until the rice is tender and the liquid is absorbed, about 10 minutes.

■ *3.* In a small bowl, sprinkle the gelatin over the half-and-half and set aside 5 minutes to soften. Stir the sugar and gelatin mixture into the hot rice mixture until the gelatin is dissolved. Turn into a 2-quart bowl and refrigerate 35 to 40 minutes, or until the mixture has just started to set.

1 cup water

¾ cup short or medium grain white rice

½ vanilla bean, split

¼ teaspoon salt

2 cups milk

½ cup dried sour cherries, blueberries, or cranberries

1 envelope unflavored gelatin

1 cup half-and-half

¼ cup sugar

½ cup heavy cream, whipped

¼ cup seedless red raspberry preserves

■ *4.* Meanwhile, melt the preserves and pour into a 1½-quart decorative mold. Set aside at room temperature to cool slightly. As the preserves cool, tip the mold so that the top one-fourth of the mold is coated with preserves.

■ *5.* When the rice mixture has just started to gel, fold in the whipped cream and spoon into the prepared mold. Cover and refrigerate 4 to 6 hours or until completely set. To unmold, dip mold into a bowl of warm water several times until sides start to loosen. Unmold onto a serving plate. Place in the refrigerator for 10 minutes for surface to harden before serving.

## PERFECT RICE PUDDING

*Using short or medium grain rice is the secret to a perfectly creamy rice pudding. It also ensures that the rice in the pudding will not get crunchy (retrograde) when refrigerated.*

# glorified rice

*This recipe is based on one found in a 1936 rice cookbook. The old-fashioned recipe calls for canned fruit cocktail or pineapple tidbits. We especially like a combination of fresh berries and seedless grapes.*

*6 servings*

■ *1.* Bring the milk, rice, and salt to a boil in a heavy 2-quart saucepan. Cook 10 minutes over low heat, stirring occasionally. Stir in the sugar, and cook 10 minutes longer over very low heat, until the rice is tender and the milk is absorbed. Stir in the almond extract, then cool to room temperature.

■ *2.* Fold in the fruit, marshmallows, if desired, and almonds. In a small bowl, with an electric mixer, beat the cream until stiff peaks form. Fold the whipped cream into the rice mixture. Turn into a serving dish. Cover and refrigerate until ready to serve.

2 cups milk

½ cup short or medium grain white rice

¼ teaspoon salt

¼ cup sugar

½ teaspoon almond extract

2 cups diced fresh or canned fruit

12 large marshmallows (optional)

½ cup coarsely chopped unblanched almonds

1 cup (½ pint) heavy cream

# rice and pineapple fritters

*18 fritters, 6 servings*

■ *1.* Drain the pineapple, collecting the juice in a measuring cup. Coarsely chop the pineapple chunks. Measure ½ cup pineapple juice and add water, if necessary, to make ½ cup.

■ *2.* Combine the flour, rice bran, granulated sugar, baking powder, cinnamon, allspice, and salt in a medium bowl. Stir in the reserved pineapple juice and the egg to make a smooth batter. Fold in the rice and pineapple.

■ *3.* Heat ½ inch of oil in a large skillet. Drop the batter into the oil, a heaping tablespoon at a time, and fry until golden on one side. Turn and fry until golden on the other side, about 5 or 6 minutes in all. Remove the fritters from the oil with a slotted spoon and drain well. Serve immediately, sprinkled with confectioners' sugar.

1 8-ounce can pineapple chunks in unsweetened pineapple juice

¾ cup all-purpose flour

¼ cup rice bran

3 tablespoons granulated sugar

1 teaspoon baking powder

½ teaspoon ground cinnamon

¼ teaspoon ground allspice

¼ teaspoon salt

1 egg

½ cup cooked brown or white rice (pages 16, 14)

Rice bran oil or vegetable oil for frying

Confectioners' sugar

# rice cheesecake

*With rice replacing some of the cream cheese, our cheesecake is lower in cholesterol and fat than the traditional cake.*

*8 servings*

- *1.* Preheat the oven to 325°F. Lightly grease an 8-inch springform pan.
- *2.* In a medium bowl, beat the cream cheese and sugar until fluffy with an electric mixer. Beat in the eggs, one at a time. Fold in the yogurt, lime or lemon juice, and rind. To have the rice visible in the cheesecake, simply fold in rice. For a cake with the texture of regular cheesecake, place the rice and cheese mixture into the container of a food processor and process with a chopping blade until smooth. Turn the mixture into the springform pan.
- *3.* Bake for 45 minutes or until the center is almost set. Turn off the oven and allow the cake to sit in the closed oven for 45 minutes. Remove the cake from the oven and cool completely on a wire rack. Remove the rim from the

2 8-ounce packages cream cheese, softened

⅓ cup sugar

2 eggs

8 ounces vanilla lowfat yogurt

2 tablespoons freshly squeezed lime or lemon juice

2 teaspoons grated lime or lemon rind

2 cups cooked medium or short grain white rice (page 14), cold

pan, cover the cake, and refrigerate several hours before cutting. Store in the refrigerator; use within 3 days.

*For an easy-to-make, fresh fruit topping, wash and thoroughly dry 2 cups of fresh raspberries, blueberries, or small strawberries. Arrange berries on top of the cheesecake. Just before serving, brush tops of berries with 2 tablespoons melted currant jelly.*

*An even easier, but perhaps more decadent, topping is made by melting ½ cup semisweet chocolate chips and drizzling the chocolate over the top of the cake. This will harden when refrigerated, so it is best to do it just before serving the cake.*

# cookies, breads, and muffins

*"A meal without rice is like a beautiful woman with only one eye."*

Ancient Chinese Proverb

# rice bran
# molasses cookies

*2 dozen*

■ *1.* Preheat the oven to 350°F. Lightly grease 2 baking sheets.

■ *2.* In a small bowl, stir together the flour, bran, baking soda, baking powder, cinnamon, ginger, cloves, and salt.

■ *3.* In a large bowl beat the brown sugar and oil with an electric mixer until well mixed. Beat in the egg and molasses. On low speed beat in the flour mixture and the raisins.

■ *4.* Drop batter by heaping teaspoonfuls onto the greased baking pans. Sprinkle tops with granulated sugar. Bake 10 to 12 minutes or until the centers feel firm when gently pressed. Remove from the pans to a wire rack to cool completely. Store in an airtight container.

1½ cups all-purpose flour

½ cup rice bran or rice polish

1 teaspoon baking soda

½ teaspoon baking powder

1 teaspoon ground cinnamon

½ teaspoon ground ginger

¼ teaspoon ground cloves

¼ teaspoon salt

½ cup firmly packed light brown sugar

⅓ cup rice bran oil or vegetable oil

1 egg or 2 egg whites

½ cup light molasses

½ cup raisins

Granulated sugar

# almond
# shortbread
# cookies

*About 4½ dozen*

- *1.* Preheat the oven to 325°F. Lightly grease 2 baking sheets.
- *2.* In a medium bowl, beat together the butter, sugar, and vanilla and almond extracts with an electric mixer. On low speed, beat in the flour, almonds, and salt, just until combined.
- *3.* Form the dough into a flattened ball and roll between pieces of floured wax paper until ⅛ inch thick. Using 2-inch cookie cutters, cut out as many cookies as possible. Reroll dough scraps and cut out more. Place the cookies on the greased baking sheets and bake 12 to 15 minutes or until the edges just start to brown. Cool on a wire rack.
- *4.* If desired, dip one end of each cookie in melted chocolate or drizzle some chocolate over top. Chill 5 minutes to set chocolate. Store cookies in a tight container in a cool, dry place.

8 tablespoons (1 stick) unsalted butter

¼ cup sugar

2 teaspoons vanilla extract

1 teaspoon almond extract

1½ cups rice flour

½ cup finely chopped unblanched almonds

¼ teaspoon salt

½ cup chocolate chips, melted (optional)

# crunchy rice squares

*16 servings*

■ *1.* Lightly brush a 9-inch square baking pan with some of the butter.

■ *2.* Combine the remaining butter and the marshmallows in a 3-quart saucepan. Warm over very low heat, stirring occasionally, until the marshmallows are melted. Stir in the vanilla and salt. Quickly stir in the cereal, candy, if desired, and nuts until the cereal is well coated with the marshmallow.

■ *3.* Turn the mixture into the buttered pan, cover with wax paper, and press until the surface is even. Cool on a wire rack for 15 minutes. Cut into squares and cool completely. Store in an airtight container.

**Variation:** Melt ½ cup semisweet chocolate chips with the marshmallows and butter before adding the cereal and nuts.

3 tablespoons unsalted butter, melted

35 large marshmallows

1 teaspoon vanilla extract

⅛ teaspoon salt

4 cups crispy rice cereal

½ cup candy-coated chocolate or peanut butter candies (optional)

½ cup coarsely chopped walnuts, pecans, or peanuts

# rice corn bread

*A favorite in turn-of-the-century menus, this moist and hearty corn bread deserves a revival.*

*9 servings*

- *1.* Preheat the oven to 400°F. Lightly grease an 8-inch square baking pan.
- *2.* Combine the flour, cornmeal, baking powder, sugar, and salt in a medium bowl. Make a well in the center. In a small bowl, combine the milk, egg, and oil, then stir into the four mixture. Stir in the rice and, if desired, the raisins. Turn the mixture into the greased pan.
- *3.* Bake for 20 to 25 minutes, or until golden brown on top and the center is firm when gently pressed.
- *4.* Cool for 10 minutes in the pan on wire rack, then cut into 9 squares and serve warm.

¾ cup all-purpose flour

¾ cup yellow cornmeal

4 teaspoons baking powder

1 teaspoon sugar

½ teaspoon salt

1 cup milk

1 egg

¼ cup rice bran oil or vegetable oil

2 cups cooked white or brown rice (pages 14, 16)

⅓ cup raisins (optional)

# rice-meal bread

*9 servings*

■ *1.* Preheat the oven to 375°F. Grease an 8-inch square baking pan.

■ *2.* In a medium bowl, combine the flour, rice meal, rice bran, sugar, baking powder, and salt.

■ *3.* In a small bowl, combine the milk, egg, oil, and pepper, if desired. Add to the dry ingredients and stir just until combined. The batter should still be a bit lumpy. Spoon the batter into the prepared pan.

■ *4.* Bake for 25 to 30 minutes or until the center is firm when gently pressed. Remove to a wire rack to cool for 5 minutes. Cut the bread into 9 squares and serve warm.

¾ cup all-purpose flour

¾ cup rice meal (see note, page 65)

¼ cup rice bran or rice polish

2 tablespoons sugar

4 teaspoons baking powder

½ teaspoon salt

1 cup milk

1 egg, beaten

2 tablespoons rice bran oil or vegetable oil

½ teaspoon cracked black pepper (optional)

# rice bran
# muffins

*Ten 2-inch muffins*

■ *1.* Preheat the oven to 350°F. Grease ten 2-inch muffin cups.

■ *2.* Combine the flour, rice bran, sugar, baking powder, baking soda, cinnamon, and salt in a medium bowl. In a small bowl, combine the buttermilk, egg, oil, and vanilla.

■ *3.* Add the buttermilk mixture to the flour mixture and stir just until combined. Do not overmix; the batter should be lumpy. Fold in the fruit.

■ *4.* Divide the batter among the greased muffin cups. Fill any empty cups with water. Bake for 20 to 25 minutes or until the centers spring back when gently pressed.

1¼ cups all-purpose flour

¾ cup rice bran or rice polish

¼ cup sugar

1½ teaspoons baking powder

½ teaspoon baking soda

½ teaspoon ground cinnamon

¼ teaspoon salt

1 cup buttermilk

1 egg, lightly beaten

2 tablespoons vegetable oil

½ teaspoon vanilla extract

½ cup blueberries, raspberries, or peeled and chopped apple

# rice bran scones

*6 scones*

■ *1.* Preheat the oven to 400°F. Grease a baking sheet.

■ *2.* In a medium bowl, stir together the flour, rice bran, sugar, baking powder, and salt.

■ *3.* In a small bowl, beat together the milk and oil. Add to the dry ingredients and stir just until combined. Add the raisins and knead the mixture into a ball.

■ *4.* On a lightly floured surface, shape the dough into a flat 8-inch round. Cut into 6 wedges. Sprinkle with cinnamon sugar, if desired. Separate wedges and place on the baking sheet.

■ *5.* Bake the scones for 18 to 20 minutes, or until browned at the edges and firm to the touch. Serve warm.

1¾ cups all-purpose flour

½ cup rice bran

1 tablespoon sugar

2 teaspoons baking powder

½ teaspoon salt

⅔ cup milk

¼ cup rice bran oil or vegetable oil

¼ cup raisins

Cinnamon sugar (optional)

# mail order sources

Conrad Rice Mill
P. O. Box 296
New Iberia, LA 70560
(318) 364-7274
1-800-551-3245 (outside Louisiana)
*Rice and rice products.*

Farms of Texas Co.
P. O. Box 1305
Alvin, TX 77512
1-800-232-Rice
*Producers of Texmati, a U.S.
aromatic rice.*

Lundberg Family Farms
P. O. Box 369
Richvale, CA 95974-0369
(916) 882-4551
*Specialty California rice and
Rizcous (rice couscous)*

The Sausage Maker
177–29 Military Road
Buffalo, New York 14207
(716) 876-5521
*Casings and sausage-making
equipment.*

Select Origins, Inc.
P. O. Box N
Southampton, NY 11968
(516) 924-5447
1-800-822-2092 (outside New York)
*Rice bran oil as well as many variet-
ies of imported and U.S. rice.*

Walnut Acres
Penns Creek, PA 17862
1-800-433-3998
*Rice and rice products.*

# index

chicken (*continued*)
  chicken gumbo, 51
  elaborate paella, 58–59
  with rice dumplings, 64–65
  chicken liver/gizzard, dirty rice, 96
chili
  basic recipe, 60
  rice balls, 26–27
Chinese fried rice, 99
chocolate
  chocolate rice pudding, 109
  topping for cheesecake, 117
cholesterol, lowering and rice, 4–5
clams
  elaborate paella, 58–59
  quick paella, 56
coconut milk, basic preparation, 98
coconut rice, 98
confetti rice salad, 43
converted rice, 9–10
  quick paella, 56
cookies
  almond shortbread cookies, 120
  crunchy rice squares, 121
  molasses cookies, 119
corn, wild rice and corn custard, 102
cornbread, rice corn bread, 122
couscous
  lamb couscous, 52–53
  *See also* rice couscous
crab
  chicken and crab pilau, 47
  Lisa Dishman's casserole, 61
crawfish tails, Lisa Dishman's casse-
    role, 61
crunchy rice squares, 121
curried dishes
  curried rice salad, 42
  kedgeree, 73
  shrimp pulao, 66
custard, wild rice and corn custard,
    102

## D

desserts
  glorified rice, 114

rice cheesecake, 116–117
rice and pineapple fritters, 115
*See also* puddings
dirty rice, 96
dumplings, rice dumplings, 64–65

## E

eggs
  kedgeree, 73
  sausage frittata, 72
enriched rice, 8–9
escarole, minestra, 22

## F

firmer rice, adjustment for, 14
freezing rice, 7
fried rice, 99
frittata
  ratatouille frittata, 72
  sausage frittata, 72
fritters, rice and pineapple fritters,
    115
fruit
  glorified rice dessert, 114
  topping for cheesecake, 117

## G

garam masala
  ingredients of, 67
  substitute for, 67
glorified rice dessert, 114
glutinous rice, 10, 12
  basic preparation of, 35
Greek-style rice salad, 38–39
green rice, 94
green risotto, 86

## H

ham hocks, red beans and rice,
    54–55
hard rice, troubleshooting, 8
harvest festivals, types of, 27
Hoppin' John, 100–101

132